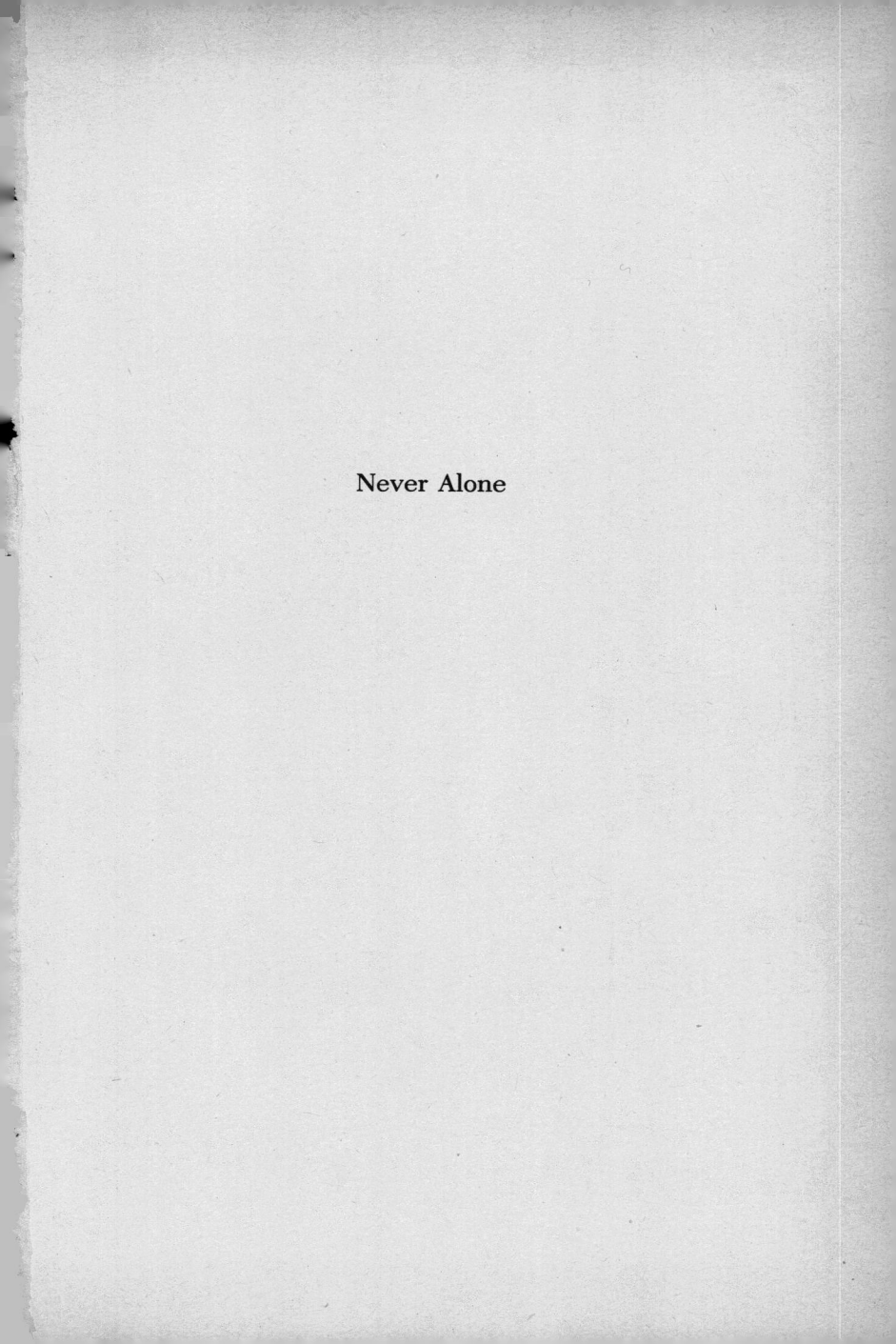

Never Alone

Never Alone
Billy K. Smith

Broadman Press
Nashville, Tennessee

© Copyright 1978 • Broadman Press.

All rights reserved.

4252-62

ISBN: 0-8054-5262-1

Dewey Decimal Classification: 223.2

Subject Heading: BIBLE—OLD TESTAMENT PSALMS

Library of Congress Catalog Card Number: 77-91272

Printed in the United States of America

Dedicated to

Irlene

my wife for thirty years
with whom I have never been lonely
and
to our five children

Ken

David

Joyce

Philip

Debra

who have helped us learn
that parents who trust God
need never feel alone

Preface

The idea for a manuscript on one of the dominant themes in the book of Psalms developed from a real-life situation. In an effort to state what the Psalms are and how they were used by Israel, I explained to my class in Introduction to the Old Testament that they developed from personal experience. Subsequently they were used in private and public worship. Then I spoke of a prevailing theme in the book: the presence of God. Through whatever experience the psalmist was going, he regularly sensed that God was with him. God was not away in the heavens unaware, unconcerned, and unavailable. Rather, he manifested himself wherever the psalmist was. Whatever his circumstances, he was never alone.

A few days later one of the students from the class invited me to hold a Bible conference in his church. When I raised the question about the book he wanted to use, he suggested the Psalms. More than that, he recalled the statement in the Old Testament class and suggested that I prepare a conference around that theme. I titled it "The Presence of God in Everyday Life." After considering several titles for this book, I settled on *Never Alone*.

My hope in sending this book out is that it might find many of God's people who are wrestling with the problems of everyday life and somehow bring the awareness of God's presence there. That may sound impersonal. It may appear to make such people too shadowy, nameless, and faceless. But hopefully I have ministered personally to enough people whose names, addresses, and circumstances I could recite that the ring of reality will come through. Like Ezekiel's dry bones, as the reader shares in the psalmists' insights, there may come a rattling and a coming together of the bones. Sinews, flesh, and skin may cover them. Breath may come into them, and they may live and stand upon their feet, flesh-and-blood reality.

Appreciation has been expressed for the origin of the idea for the book. But without the input of many people into my life, the book could not have been written. Among the more significant contributors were three professors: J. Wash Watts, who taught me Hebrew; J. Hardee Kennedy, who taught me to love the Psalms; and John Olen Strange, who by example taught me compassion for people (in addition to a considerable amount of course material). I mention these not to implicate them for any of the weaknesses of this work, but to express sincere gratitude for their labors in my life.

Irlene, my wife, checked the copy and offered pertinent suggestions. Her insights, skills, and encouragement were of inestimable help. Brenda Murfin, my secretary, spent hours typing and retyping the manuscript. For her patience and persistence I am grateful. My children were considerate of my time during the critical days of completing the work and meeting the due date for the manuscript. I offer them my sincere thanks.

Churches where I have ministered as pastor have afforded years of experience in sharing with the members the problems, burdens, and blessings of life. By such ministry, insight into the need for practical application of the principles contained in the Psalms was gained. Among those churches were: Society Hill Baptist Church, Oakvale, Mississippi;

PREFACE

Monte Sano Baptist Church, Baton Rouge, Louisiana; First Baptist Church, Homer, Louisiana; and First Baptist Church, Alvin, Texas.

Unless otherwise indicated the Revised Standard Version is the translation employed throughout the book. Occasionally the King James Version is cited for comparative study. In a few instances a literal rendering of the original language is used in an effort to open up the essential idea in a word or phrase.

Many people have contributed to my understanding of the Psalms and to my understanding of life. Some I have never seen but feel I know through their writings. I have tried to give credit for that which I consciously borrowed from others. But to give precise credit to all who have shaped my thinking is as impossible as unscrambling eggs. My hope is that this combination of thoughts, pulled from many sources, will make a worthy contribution to the lives of all who use their time to read it.

BILLY K. SMITH

Introduction

The Psalms are hymns, prayers, and poems out of the real-life experiences of the authors. Kyle Yates wrote: "Any experience in a man's life can find its picture in these ageless poems. The solution for all of life's problems can be discovered in these pages." [1] Out of personal experience in reading the Psalms, A. Leonard Griffith concluded: "No collection of writings in all the world so completely covers the whole range of God's activity in man's experience. Every man can find himself somewhere in the Book of Psalms." [2]

Billy Graham has said that he reads the Psalms devotionally to bring him into the presence of God. I know of no other Scriptures as capable of creating the consciousness of God's presence as a careful reading of the Psalms. H. C. Leupold asserted that "the psalms continually carry the reader into the immediate presence of God. They do not refer to Him in the abstract. God is not a God of the distance to the psalmist." [3] Although God transcends creation, he condescends to manifest his presence in the daily experiences of his people.

The most urgent need of believers in God is assurance of his presence. Anything is bearable if we are confident that God is with us, that we do not have to bear it alone. When our enemies assail us, it is reassuring to remember that God is our ally. When death approaches, it is comforting to realize that the author and sustainer of life is near. When sickness shatters our world, it can be put back together with a moment's meditation on the ministry of the attending Great Physician. When sin makes us unclean, burdens us with guilt, and robs us of joy, it is cleansing, lifting, and joy-restoring to be in the presence of our forgiving God. How comforting to know that whatever trials or triumphs come to the child of God, he is never alone! The chorus of a familiar hymn expresses this confidence thus: "No never alone, no never alone./He promised never to leave me,/ never to leave me alone."

The psalms selected for consideration represent a relatively wide range of experiences common to man in the last quarter of the twentieth century. The order of treatment is not necessarily suggestive of a logical sequence. The only exception would be the first chapter. It should be read first, for it establishes the thesis of the book. God is not absent but present. He is not inaccessible but available. After reading the first chapter, the reader might as profitably read the fifth chapter as the second chapter.

These psalms are representative of the kinds of materials found in this portion of the Scriptures. Each psalm in its own way carries the overarching theme, *never alone.* Hopefully the result of this study will be a growing fellowship with God on a day-to-day basis and a growing appreciation and use of the psalms to voice praise and prayer to God. The poet understood the value of God's presence daily. He suggests an approach to ensure the reality and the recognition of his presence each day.

His Presence Came Like Sunrise

I met God in the morning,
  When my day was at its best,

And His presence came like sunrise,
    Like a glory in my breast.

All day long the presence lingered;
    All day long He stayed with me;
And we sailed in perfect calmness
    O'er a very troubled sea.

Other ships were blown and battered,
    Other ships were sore distressed,
But the winds that seemed to drive them
    Brought to us a peace and rest.

Then I thought of other mornings,
    With a keen remorse of mind,
When I too had loosed the moorings
    With the presence left behind.

So I think I know the secret,
    Learned from many a troubled way;
You must seek him in the morning,
    If you want him through the day.[4]

Contents

1. Where Is Your God? 17
2. When Prayers Seem Blocked 28
3. When Doubts Arise 42
4. When Troubles Come 52
5. When Sickness Strikes 61
6. When Fears Dismay 72
7. When Guilt Overwhelms 85
8. When Needs Are Numerous 98
9. When Praise Is Missing 111

1
Where Is Your God?

Psalms 42 and 43

The title of J. B. Phillips' book *Your God Is Too Small* sets forth his thesis that men often limit God by their narrow-gauged conceptions of him. To some he is God-in-a-box. To others he is a Resident Policeman, a Parental Hangover, a Pale Galilean, or the Meek and Mild God.[1]

Many in our day would restrict God to a building, to a day, even to one hour on Sunday morning. I have not found God that manageable, that easy to pigeonhole. Some of the psalms seem to limit God to a house—the temple. Even in this psalm the psalmist was remembering the joys of corporate worship at the temple. But it is the God of the temple, not the temple itself, for which the psalmist longed (Ps. 139:7-12; 1 Kings 8:27).

When things are going well, we tend to conclude that God is with us. But when trouble comes, we are prone to equate that with God's absence. The psalmist wrestled with this problem. His enemies observed his troubles and his tears and questioned, "Where is your God?" The implication was that if his God were present, his troubles would have fled away.

The most pressing problem Job faced was not his devastating calamities but his sense of abandonment. He felt forsaken not only by man but also by God. His painful plea was, "Oh, that I knew where I might find him,/that I might come even to his seat!" (Job 23:3). The psalmist, too, felt cut off from God. Perhaps he had been ill and thus was unable to make the usual pilgrimage to Jerusalem. It may have been that his duty as a soldier prohibited his participation in temple worship. Whatever the explanation, the psalmist felt separated from God. His response was expressed in terms of physical thirst. He longed for God as the hart longs for streams with water.

Intense Longings, 42:1–3

1. *A Graphic Analogy* (vv. 1–2)

The psalm opens with a vivid picture taken from the animal world. It was the dry season of the year. The wadies of the tableland of Palestine were arid, and one stream after another had run dry. A hind (female deer) with parched tongue stood between the rocks, panting for water. She had made a long journey in search for water, only to find a dry hole. For the psalmist this pictured his spiritual thirst for God. Some commentators find in this psalm a longing for the sanctuary. Others emphasize the fact that the longing is for God himself. Both go together, though the longing for God is paramount (v. 1). Love for the sanctuary without love for the God of the sanctuary is meaningless. Love for God which does not result in love for his house is unnatural.

Do you know what it is to thirst for God? Could it be that men and women thirst for him without understanding the nature of that inner longing? What about the prodigal son (who spent all in riotous living) or the woman at the well (who lusted for one more man)—do you suppose they were actually thirsting for God?

"Living God" sets the psalmist's God over against the lifeless idols worshiped by the pagans (Jer. 2:13). The meaning may be "the God of my life" as in verse 8—that is, the life-giving God. This may hint at the psalmist's problem—

intense longing for the life-giving God in the face of the approach of death-dealing disease. Kyle Yates wrote, "The psalmist is almost certainly suffering from some human ailment that makes him a loathsome object, visible to men who can taunt him with the hastily conceived conclusion that his God has forgotten him." [2]

Some commentators follow the suggested emendation in the margin so as to read "appear" instead of "see" in verse 2. The Niphal of the verb *see* has the meaning *appear* in many contexts (Ex. 23:15,17; 34:23 f.; Deut. 16:16). Thus, no emendation is necessary. In this context "appear" is the correct rendering. The form of expression "appear before God's face" implies going to the sanctuary. Whatever had hindered attendance at the sanctuary service had brought about the feeling of separation from God. It was not that the psalmist could not have felt the nearness of God without going to the sanctuary, but under those circumstances the two things went together.

Isaiah invited all who thirst to find fulfillment in God (Isa. 55:1–2). A hymn describes the satisfaction of soul thirst:

> I heard the voice of Jesus say,
> "Come unto Me and rest;
> Lay down, thou weary one,
> lay down Thy head upon My breast."
> I came to Jesus as I was,
> Weary, and worn, and sad;
> I found in Him a resting place,
> And He has made me glad.
> I heard the voice of Jesus say,
> "Behold I freely give
> The living water; thirsty one,
> Stoop down and drink and live."
> I came to Jesus, and I drank
> Of that life-giving stream;
> My thirst was quenched, my soul revived,
> And now I live in Him.[3]

2. A *Grief-ridden Anxiety* (v. 3a)

The precise cause of the tears of the psalmist and the taunts of unidentified persons is not revealed. The circumstances seemed to say that God had forgotten or forsaken the psalmist. Whatever the problem, it was not one which had just arisen. For days and nights the psalmist had done more weeping than eating. Perhaps some disease caused him completely to lose his appetite. He was depressed and discouraged that God was silent and absent. His pitiful circumstances seemed to contradict his profession of faith in God.

Sometimes the flow of tears so blurs vision that a person is unable to catch even the faintest glimpse of God in his suffering or sorrow. We say to a crying child, anxious over the seriousness of an injury sustained in an accident, "Dry your tears and look. It's not a very bad cut." Many adults, overcome with anxious grief over their distressing circumstances, need encouragement to dry their weeping eyes and look at the evidences of God's love and care.

3. *A Grave Accusation* (v. 3b)

In the face of natural calamities, we question, *Where is God in all of this?* When social injustice grinds the face of the poor into the dust, we wonder, *Why doesn't God do something?* The psalmist (Ps. 10:1–4) accused the Lord of standing "afar off" and hiding himself "in times of trouble." His day was so dark and his eyes were so blind that he could not see the hand of God in what was happening.

"Where is your God?" is the taunting question of an unidentified "they" here, but referred to as "my adversaries" in verse 10. Leonard Griffith points out that we are not concerned with the question of whether God exists, but rather with what God is doing—or more precisely, *Where*

WHERE IS YOUR GOD?

has God gone? Griffith continues:

> The Creator and Ruler of the universe, call him a Supreme Being or Being Itself, is too often conspicuous by his absence. Sometimes this world seems such an undisciplined madhouse and our personal lives so utterly at the mercy of blind fate that we are tempted to echo the bitter complaint of H. G. Wells, who said of God that "he is an ever-absent help in time of trouble." [4]

While "Where is your God?" was the question of his adversaries, the psalmist must have wondered about it also. Had God forgotten him? Why was he allowing such suffering? Why did God not come to his rescue? As the taunt implied, was the psalmist really a God-forsaken man?

Inspiring Memories, 42:4–8

1. *Thrill of the Throng* (v. 4)

Memory of the past revived the psalmist's languishing soul. His leadership of a throng of worshipers may have been in the role of a musician, a player of the lyre (43:4). Whatever his role, he recalled what a blessed experience the festivals at the sanctuary were in former times. He remembered the glad music, the crowding worshipers, the godly souls who walked the sacred courts, the lavish offerings, the fervent prayers, the sense of the divine presence, and the thrill of divine forgiveness. Nothing could snatch away these precious realities of the past.

Hope sprung up within the psalmist's soul as he remembered God. But just now he was remembering the throng of worshipers gathering to celebrate some religious festival. He was part of that throng. He was leading them. He heard their glad shouts and their songs of thanksgiving. He was no spectator, no sideliner. He was in their midst singing, shouting, celebrating. He was buoyed up by their jubilant faith. He might question his own soul, but the affirmations of the multitude could not be disputed. Corporate worship has rewards which cannot be received from private devotions.

Modern pilgrims who deliberately cut themselves off from frequent experiences of corporate worship risk the same feeling of abandonment by God. Thinking one can grow and be a fruitful Christian cut off from the body of Christ is as ridiculous as looking for a red, juicy apple on an apple limb severed from the tree. Faith inspires faith. The presence of other people singing and praising God prods one to participate in worship. Such worship strengthens the conviction that God is real and present.

2. *Hope in the Helper* (vv. 5–6a)

The psalmist addressed his own lagging soul with a challenging question: "Why are you cast down, O my soul,/and why are you disquieted within me?" *Your past experience should prove that God has not abandoned you; you really have no grounds for discouragement and doubt,* he told himself. In a positive admonition the psalmist urged his soul to wait and trust and hope in God. He expected to praise God again for his help. At least God was the one to whom the psalmist turned. The author was well on the way to recovery when he offered a frank confession that he was "cast down" (v. 6). But he was confident that remembering God would aid in recovery. His help was in God.

This is not whistling in the dark. Hope is the laying of a bridge from the past to the future. That bridge is anchored to the past by remembering God, by recalling his help in the past. In the midst of the throng of worshipers, God had manifested himself. But all of that is past tense. Now the psalmist was absent from the throng. Now God seemed far away. But the other end of his bridge was nailed down securely to the future, when he would again praise God. In the meantime he would hope, not whistle in the dark. His

WHERE IS YOUR GOD?

hope was anchored in recollection on one end and expectation on the other.

3. *Triumph over Trouble* (vv. 7–8)

The overwhelming trouble the psalmist faced is described in terms of wave after never-ending wave of the waters of a cataract closing over him. That which encouraged him in the face of imminent death was the steadfast love of God by day and the fact that in the dark watches of the night God gives a song. Does trouble drive you to despair, or does it drive you to your knees in prayer? The psalmist prayed to "the God of my life" (v. 8). It was when the psalmist remembered God, his steadfast love, his song in the night, and his answer to prayer, that he triumphed over trouble. The poet found in Jesus the answer to the psalmist's prayer:

> I heard the voice of Jesus say,
> "I am this dark world's Light;
> Look unto Me; thy morn shall rise,
> And all thy day be bright."
> I looked to Jesus, and I found
> In Him my Star, my Sun;
> And in that Light of life I'll walk
> Till traveling days are done.[5]

Insistent Questions, 42:9–11

1. *Addressed to God* (v. 9)

God as his "rock" was the firm ground on which the psalmist's whole life rested. However, the current circumstances perplexed him. His feelings, his faith, and the facts didn't square. His faith asserted, *God is my rock.* The facts responded, *If so, where is he?* His feelings were confused by the conflict between his faith and the facts. Thus, in question he expressed his feelings, "Why go I mourning/because of the oppression of the enemy?" Why should I let the enemy get me down when I've got a Rock to hold me up?

2. *Asked by the Adversaries* (v. 10)

Most men have found the taunts of their fellowmen the most bitter of human experiences. My son, Philip, was torn between a decision to stay with the baseball team with which he had practiced for three weeks or to join a new team being formed on the seminary campus. The hardest part of the decision had to do with what his friends on campus would say if he chose to stay with the team at Harris playground. Even the words of friends can hurt.

Little children chant, "Sticks and stones may break my bones, but words will never hurt me." That isn't true. Words do hurt. With but a word aflame with anger, an otherwise good day may go up in smoke.

Words are fraught with awesome power for good and evil. Just a word of encouragement may bolster the lagging spirit of a weary pilgrim. But just as surely a discouraging word may take all the wind out of the sails of one who is enjoying a great day.

The taunts of one's enemies are like deadly wounds (Hebrew, "killing"). These are the kinds of wounds that don't bleed. But the person who is the brunt of such attacks is quite sure the jugular vein is cut and his life is fading fast away, blood or no blood. Such taunts eat a man up. They are like a torment in the bones, whether they come from friends or foes. What the psalmist's adversaries asked was, "Where is your God?" Is he asleep? busy? disinterested? weak? away? What's the problem? Has God forgotten? Such questions can be quite upsetting when asked continually.

3. *Aimed at Self* (v. 11; 43:2,5)

The repeated refrain is not simply repeated with no progress being made. Deep distress, doubt, and discouragement dominated the first appearance of the refrain. This time it expresses an emerging certainty, "for I shall again praise him." The final use in 43:5 is the climax of returning confidence in God, "who is the help of my countenance" (author's paraphrase). The psalmist was certain that his waiting for God would not be in vain. Thus, the final result of the question addressed to his soul was a climb out of stormy unrest, out of soul agony, to a strange stillness that ended in indescribable joy.

Though talking to oneself is not usually considered a sign of mental health, if a man is cast down he might do well to try it. Especially if he raises the right questions and finds the right answers is this a good, therapeutic procedure. Why are you cast down? Is your life anchored in God? Can memory enable you to recapture past confidence in God? What never happened can't be remembered. But if help from God in past crises can be recollected, hope for help from God in the future can reasonably be expected.

Entreating Prayers, 43:1-4

1. *For Defense* (v. 1*a*)

This section is permeated by the spirit of prayer. The first request was for vindication of the good name of the psalmist, now sullied by the slurs and taunts of his adversaries. He knew he was innocent, that his illness did not condemn him as one forsaken of God. So confident was he that he was willing to submit to the penetrating inspection of God. To call on God to vindicate him was to declare his own sense of worthiness. Men look on the outside, but God looks at the heart. The psalmist was asserting, *My heart is clean*.

Using another figure, he was ready to retain God as his competent lawyer to take the case to court. He called on God to "defend his cause" against an ungodly people. Here the emphasis seems to be on their great numbers and their attitude of ungodliness. Paul suggested that it was ludicrous to imagine anyone bringing a charge against God's elect. God is the one who justifies them. Where in all the universe is one who could successfully condemn the Christian? Certainly not Christ. He is the one who died, rose, and reigns to make intercession in our behalf (Rom. 8:31-33).

2. *For Deliverance* (v. 1*b*)

Feeling he was under the dominance of "deceitful and unjust men," the psalmist prayed for deliverance. Not only did he want to clear his name, but also he longed to be cut loose from his adversaries' power. He wanted to be free of his disease and free of their taunts. A primary reason many Christians remain shackled to sin is that they don't want to be liberated. They are enjoying the pleasures of sin.

Jesus asked the blind man in Jericho, "What do you want me to do for you?" (Matt. 20:32). The answer should have been obvious. The man was blind, wasn't he? Yet Jesus asked. Perhaps Jesus was making sure that he really wanted to see. He might see some things that would disturb him. He might see some things which would call for his responsible involvement. Doubtless many people today are more secure in their blindness or poverty or other handicap than they would be if liberated and expected to do something daring and bold about the problems of humanity.

The basis for the psalmist's appeal to God for defense and deliverance was that God is "the God who is my refuge." It appeared to his antagonists and to himself that God had cast him off. Though he did not understand it, the psalmist turned to God, his refuge, and presented his painful why to him. If God answered, the answer is not recorded. And yet the answer of the psalmist to his own question was his faith-step in fleeing to God, his refuge, and leaving his painful question with God, assured of an answer of eternal truth.

3. *For Direction* (vv. 3-4)

Darkness had settled upon the psalmist. He had lost his way. He prayed for direction. He requested that God's "light" and "truth" be sent out to guide him to God's "holy hill," his "dwelling." If a man is really lost and shrouded in darkness, running faster won't help. That only accelerates the pace and increases the probability of a catastrophe. What's needed is light to dispel the darkness and truth to mark the way.

What the psalmist yearned for was not simply his presence in the sanctuary, but the assurance of God's presence and acceptance at the altar, the meeting place with God. "Light" may mean "steadfast love," the token of God's favor. Light and truth are envisioned as guardian angels walking along at the side of the psalmist to guide him to his desired destination, the place of reconciliation with God. He longed for more than the motions of devotion, more than another sermon. He hungered for God, his "joy." Then God would again be upon his lips. The pain of doubt would be turned into the praise of assurance.

Can God satisfy the hungering and thirsting of a man today? Jesus said, "If any one thirst, let him come to me and drink" (John 7:37). He promised, "He who comes to me shall not hunger, and he who believes in me shall never thirst" (John 6:35). And again he promised, "Whoever drinks of the water that I shall give him will never thirst; the water that I shall give him will become in him a spring of water welling up to eternal life" (John 4:14). Millions have found these claims to be true.

2
When Prayers Seem Blocked

Psalm 51

Observing Jesus at prayer, one of his disciples was inspired to request of him, "Lord, teach us to pray, as John taught his disciples" (Luke 11:1). After giving a model prayer, Jesus encouraged his disciples to be persistent in prayer: "Ask, and it will be given you; seek, and you will find; knock, and it will be opened to you" (11:9). James lamented that Christians often "have not" because they "ask not" or they "ask amiss" (Jas. 4:2–3, KJV). Prayer is conversing with our heavenly Father. Untold blessings flow from such communion.

God's problem is not giving what a believer might ask, but inducing his child to ask, believing. The attitude of prayer is the willingness to open up the lines of communication with God. But the chief hindrance to prayer is unforgiven sin. Sin unacknowledged, unconfessed, or unforgiven blocks fellowship with God. John wrote, "If we say that we have fellowship with him, and walk in darkness, we lie, and do not the truth" (1 John 1:6, KJV). Unforgiven sin leaves one feeling completely cut off from God. In such a state prayer is eliminated from the agenda of life altogether. When a right relationship is restored through confession and the granting of forgiveness, any other prayer the penitent child wants to make is possible.

The superscription states that this psalm is based on

WHEN PRAYERS SEEM BLOCKED 29

David's response to Nathan's reproof for his sin with Bathsheba. The wording indicates that the superscription is likely an editorial addition at a later date. Because of this and a number of internal matters, many commentators deny Davidic authorship of this psalm. However, all of the so-called internal evidence can be handled in a manner which favors Davidic authorship without doing violence to sound interpretation. Without being dogmatic, I accept the tradition that David wrote the psalm.

The story of David's sin, Nathan's reproof of David, the judgment of God upon David, and David's response to Nathan's reproof are all set forth in 2 Samuel 11—12. When confronted by Nathan's accusation "Thou art the man" (KJV), David did not try to justify his actions. He frankly admitted, "I have sinned against the Lord." Although Psalm 51 does not mention David's sins by name, adultery and murder, surely they explain the soul agony expressed in the psalm.

This psalm is regularly described as a penitential psalm. It is the prayer of a repentant child of God. A careful following of the steps in this prayer may suggest a pattern suitable for all prayer.

Prayer for Mercy, 51:1

1. *The Command of the Psalmist Expects It* (v. 1*a*)

The plea for mercy was based on the character of God. At the same time it was a confession of guilt. The verb form of "mercy" means to be gracious, merciful, compassionate. It is an imperative and therefore a strange command, unless one concedes that the psalmist had a true knowledge of God. He must have known that God was a God of mercy—in fact, of "abundant mercy." Use of the imperative asserts that the psalmist knew that God was ready to forgive and was happy to be commanded in accord with his will to forgive sinners and to give them a measure of his mercy.

Gaining boldness in prayer often waits on getting or regaining clear insight into the nature of God. In the aftermath of the plunge into sin, guilt rushes over one like a tidal wave. Diverted from the main problem by the battle with guilt, such a person loses perspective and forgets that God is merciful and ready to forgive. Down endless corridors he presses, intent upon finding release from the weight of guilt. Only as he remembers the mercy of God does he dare approach God at all. With remembrance comes boldness: "Have mercy!"

2. *The Confession of Sin Invites It* (v. 1c)

To cast oneself upon the mercy of God is to confess oneself to be guilty of sin. In legal proceedings to cast oneself upon the mercy of the court is to confess guilt. More than that, it is a request to do what is best for the guilty party under the circumstances. Like the publican in Jesus' story, the psalmist was so overwhelmed with the sense of sin that all he could do was plead mercy. When confronted with his heinous crimes by God's courageous prophet, David readily confessed, "I have sinned against the Lord." Now his appeal for mercy acknowledged guilt and set the stage for forgiveness.

3. *The Character of God Guarantees It* (v. 1b)

The command "have mercy" was based on the character of God, not on the merit of the supplicant. "Steadfast love" described God's loyalty to his covenant people. It was the nearest Old Testament parallel to New Testament *grace*. It was the cement which bound God to his people. After the rebellion and sin of Israel represented in the golden calf episode, the Lord renewed the broken covenant. The new relationship was to be based on the character of God, not the conduct of man. It was not "If you will obey my voice and keep my covenant" (Ex. 19:5). Instead it was "The Lord, the Lord, a God merciful and gracious, slow to anger, and abounding in steadfast love" (Ex. 34:6). It would be based on the character of God.

"Abundant mercy" is from a word that means to love tenderly, to pity, to have compassion or mercy. The word is used in Psalm 18 (v. 1) to describe David's love for the Lord. In Psalm 103 the word casts God in the role of a father who pities his children (v. 13).

"Blot out" is another imperative and is a bold command based on a clear concept of the character of God. The psalmist knew that a God characterized by great pity would be quick to respond to the command of his penitent child to "blot out" his transgression. Forgiveness is guaranteed by the character of God.

Prayer for Cleansing, 51:2–4

1. *Catalogue of Sins* (vv. 1*b*–2)

The nature of the psalmist's sin is captured in three strong words: (1) "transgression," the sin of conscious rebellion, a deliberate violation of a known standard; (2) "iniquity," moral crookedness, perversion, depravity of conduct; (3) "sin," missing the mark God set as the goal for life. What a wretched thing sin is!

David did not engage in buck-passing as Adam and Eve did in the Garden and as we are prone to do. He said what happened was "my" transgression, "my" iniquity, "my" sin. He acknowledged responsibility for it. He did not plead circumstances or implicate Bathsheba. He did not blame anyone else. He did not say, "Under the circumstances I couldn't help myself." He accepted full responsibility.

2. *Cry for Cleansing* (vv. 1*b*–2)

"Blot out" suggests erasure from a record. Moses interceded for Israel after her rebellion against God. He prayed for their forgiveness. Then he added, "If not, blot me, I pray thee, out of thy book" (Ex. 32:32). The idea is: Erase my name from your book if you can't erase their sin. God had the record of David's transgression, and only God was able to erase it from the books.

"Wash me thoroughly" pictures a woman treading the dirt out of clothes (Ex. 19:10). "Cleanse" is used of the process of removing the dross from metals (Mal. 3:3). Sin was so ugly the psalmist stacked all the strong words for sin in a pile and said, *Look at it! Isn't it awful?* Then because the strain of sin was so deep, the dirt of sin so ground in, he stacked all the strong words for cleansing in a pile and said, *It will take all these detergents to get the sin out.* Thus, the psalmist asked for complete cleansing—a clean record, a clean life, and a clear name.

3. *Cleansing of Conscience* (v. 3)

There has been a cataloging of sins and a cry for cleansing in general. Now the psalmist confessed his sins in particular. Of the three strong words for sin he chose the strongest, "rebellion," and acknowledged that as his sin. When the psalmist said, "I know," he implied he did not need to be convinced of his transgression. In fact, how could he forget? His sin was ever before him. He was constantly conscious of it. Nathan had said, "Thou art the man." David's conscience echoed, "I am the man."

Most sinners don't need to be reminded that they are sinners. They need to be referred to the Savior. Not only does he have the authority to forgive sin (Mark 2:10) but also with it the power to remove guilt. John assured us that the blood of Jesus Christ "cleanses us from all sin" (1 John

1:7). That's a phrase declaring that Jesus has the right and the resources for dealing with man's sin in general. But John followed that with a word picture, sharp as a rifle shot, charting a clear path to forgiveness of sins in particular. Look at the verbal painting, "If we confess our sins, he is faithful and just to forgive us our sins, and to cleanse us from all unrighteousness" (1 John 1:9, KJV).

"To confess" means to say the same thing. That is, as one acknowledges sin and agrees with God that his sin is sin, he is well on the way toward securing forgiveness and cleansing. As long as we excuse our sins and fail to acknowledge our sins as sin, there is no basis for forgiveness. But John assured us that our confession will let loose the floodgates of God's forgiveness. He is faithful and just. You can count on it every time. And riding on the crest of forgiveness is grace abounding to effect the cleansing of conscience, the removal of the three-thousand-pound weight of guilt.

4. *Cleansing of Attitude Toward God* (v. 4)

This verse has created problems for commentators through the years. Some say that such a statement is utterly irreconcilable with the great wrongs done to Bathsheba and to Uriah. The verse is part of the internal evidence used to deny Davidic authorship. However, as Leupold asserts, "Yet on the other hand, it is quite thinkable that the fact that all sin is, in the last analysis, sin against the Holy One Himself had hit David's conscience so hard that he voiced his conviction in this absolute statement." [1] His sin, as all sin, was primarily disobedience against God's law and therefore an offense to God. David acknowledged that God was not unrighteous in sentencing him to suffer for his sins.

Rather than blame God and justify himself, David justified God and took full blame for himself. He frankly confessed that he had "done that which is evil in thy sight." It must have been evil in David's sight also. Else he never would have confessed it, and he would not have justified God. His attitude toward God was clearing up.

Prayer for Purity, 51:5–7

1. *Tainted by Sin* (v. 5)

The word rendered "behold" is used in verse 5 and verse 6. It is an attention getter, a "listen, this is important" word. In verse 5 the psalmist confessed, "I have been a sinner from the start" (author's paraphrase). In verse 6 he acknowledged, "Thou desirest truth in the inward being;/therefore teach me wisdom in my secret heart." From the moment life began, the taint of sin was upon the psalmist. So in effect he was saying, "With sin saturating my conception and birth, you need not expect anything but sin from me." This is not to point an accusing finger at his mother, but to humble himself. It is not to excuse sin but to explain it. Paul wrote, "For all have sinned, and come short of the glory of God" (Rom. 3:23, KJV). David was saying, "I'm no exception to the rule. I'm tainted, too."

2. *Taught by God* (v. 6)

The writer admitted he was not what he ought to be. He knew what God desired him to be. He was willing to become that. Thus, he was teachable. He was saying, "I know what you desire. I know I am not that. But I am willing to become that."

Jesus taught that it was not what went into a man that defiled him, but what came out of him. Truly out of the heart arise the issues of life. Thus, truth in the inward part and wisdom in the "secret heart" are what are needed. The Lord alone is able to build these into the inner man.

WHEN PRAYERS SEEM BLOCKED

3. *Treated as Clean* (v. 7)

This is a prayer for purity, for complete cleansing (Isa. 1:18). The word translated "purge" has in it the word for sin. The thought in the word is "De-sin me." "Hyssop" was used in Jewish ceremonies of cleansing or healing from leprosy (Lev. 14) and cleansing from defilement after contact with a dead body (Num. 19:18). There is a double idea of cleansing and pronouncing clean.

"Wash" is a strong word which includes pounding, stamping, and vigorous rubbing in order to get all the dirt out. The prayer is addressed to God. When God cleanses a man, he is really clean. He is whiter than snow. It matters not how tainted with sin a man may be; the job of cleansing is not too big for God. Isaiah assures, "Though your sins are like scarlet,/they shall be as white as snow;/though they are red like crimson,/they shall become like wool" (Isa. 1:18). The only condition is "if you are willing" (Isa. 1:19). God is able!

Prayer for Joy, 51:8–12

1. *Joy Out of Chastening* (v. 8)

The expression "joy and gladness" means "deep joy." David was crushed by Nathan's indictment. But the result God envisions is joy, a joy arising out of chastening. This is the thought in the expression "let the bones which thou hast broken rejoice." The Hebrew text has "make me to hear joy and gladness" instead of "fill me." Only God could enable the psalmist to hear the music of joy and gladness in chastening. Wrongly related to the Lord, all chastening is received with sadness. The author of Hebrews quoted Proverbs 3:11–12 and explained that chastening is for our good. Then he concluded, "For the moment all discipline seems painful rather than pleasant; later it yields the peaceful fruit of righteousness" (Heb. 12:11).

2. *Joy After Atonement* (v. 9)

Two things David prayed for would bring joy to his saddened heart. First, he asked God not to look upon his sins. He wanted God to "totally disregard what the sinner is guilty of." [2] Several metaphors in the Bible express God's manner of dealing with sin when man confesses. For instance, at least once God is pictured as casting our sin behind his back. This suggests that he no longer looks upon it, that he does not charge it to our account any more. Another portrait of God has him removing our sins from us as far as the east is from the west. With the realization that God has released us from the penalty of sin comes the radiant joy of reconciliation. When relationships are restored, the joys of fellowship may be resumed.

Second, David asked God to erase his sins as the writing on a slate is erased with a wet sponge. The poet was confident that joy would return when God had taken care of his sin problem. Sin may add fun, but it always subtracts joy.

3. *Joy of a New Creation* (v. 10)

How destructive sin is! It hushes the heavenly music in the soul. It defiles the heart, the well-spring of thought and action. It corrupts the spirit. So complete is the destruction wrought by sin that God must be called in to re-create the heart and the spirit of a man. Repair won't do. A transplant is required. Here is part of the Old Testament foundation for the New Testament doctrine of a new birth. Jeremiah and Ezekiel shared these insights of need for a new birth, a new beginning (Jer. 31:33; Ezek. 36:26-27).

The clean heart the psalmist wanted must be a new creation (2 Cor. 5:17). The same word used to describe the creation of the heavens and the earth in the Genesis account is used here. It is *bara,* a verb used only with God as the subject. God alone can do what the sinner needs done—a

WHEN PRAYERS SEEM BLOCKED

clean heart, a new and right spirit. When attitude and spirit are wrong, nothing else can be right. These cast a cloud over all of a person's actions and relationships. Only the person who has experienced the creation of a clean heart and the restoration of a right spirit can know the attendant joy that floods the soul.

4. *Joy in God's Presence* (v. 11)

To be cut off from God's presence is the worst possible calamity the psalmist could imagine. God's presence is the signal of God's favor. To be cast away is to be cut off from his favor. David feared that his sins would result in a Saul-like loss of the presence of God (1 Sam. 16:1,7,14). He knew of the Lord's rejection of Saul as king. Saul had an array of outward attributes which would have seemed to commend him. But he had a heart problem. David was relayed the message that "the Lord looks on the heart."

The most crushing blow a man can receive from his fellow-man is to be rejected. Little children at play experience this. It can be shattering. To be cast off from God is even more shattering. Isaiah described the occasion of Israel's exodus from Egypt under Moses as a time when God "put in the midst of them/his holy Spirit" (Isa. 63:11). In the writer's mind the loss of the Spirit would mean the loss of grace. Access to the throne of grace means that the door is open to the source of joy.

5. *Joy of a Willing Spirit* (v. 12)

Once the poet had known the joy of God's deliverance. Now the joy was gone. Through acts of overt and blatant sin, the prison doors of bondage clanged shut upon David again. He knew the futility of grabbing the bars in an effort to extricate himself from his prison. Instead of making frantic effort to break the bars, he prayed for God's deliverance.

Notice that the wording involved reads "thy salvation."

A "willing spirit" is a spirit of willingness, an inclination to obey. A rebellious spirit had resulted in bondage to fear and sin. David yearned for freedom, for a spirit of willing service. This spirit is more nearly in accord with the state of grace. There is no joy in duty done grudgingly, unwillingly. Joy comes out of willing, obedient service. This is equally true for the pastor of a church, the teacher of a class, or a member of the choir. When a child must be coerced, a simple chore becomes a drudgery. Willing obedience puts joy in the deed.

Prayer for Usefulness, 51:13–17

The usual vow to follow a prayer like this was a thanksgiving offering. But the psalmist offered himself. He pledged (1) to teach transgressors God's way in order to turn them to God, (2) to travel around singing God's deliverance, and (3) to testify of what God desires more than sacrifice—namely, a broken and contrite heart. The psalmist offered himself with a desire to be used of God.

1. *As a Teacher* (v. 13)

The most effective teachers are those who not only know the principles of God but who also have experienced what they teach. The "then" is not in the Hebrew text, but the cohortative ending of the verb in this context may be appropriately rendered "then." Though David's acts of sin brought no honor to him, he was willing to teach other transgressors what he had learned. The sure result was the conversion of other sinners. "Thy ways" suggests that God's ways are not man's ways. What are God's ways? The ways of mercy, forgiveness, cleansing, renewal, and restoration.

Have you experienced the ways of God? You are responsible to teach them to others. One of the most rewarding exercises of a growing Christian is to share what he is learning with someone else. Everyone who is growing in grace and the knowledge of the Lord can establish a Paul-Timothy relationship with someone who needs to be taught. Such teaching regularly turns sinners to God.

2. *As a Troubadour* (v. 14)

A troubadour is a traveling ballad singer. The psalmist volunteered to sing aloud of God's deliverance. Such singing hinges on God's deliverance from "bloodguiltiness." Use of the term "bloodguiltiness" meant David saw that he shed Uriah's blood. Though the sword was in the hand of another, the lust and greed of David wielded the sword. David vowed to praise God in song for the granting of pardon. God's deliverance puts a song on the tongue of the one delivered. Do you have anything to sing about?

3. *As a Testifier* (vv. 15–17)

The psalmist vowed to praise God publicly when God enabled him to offer such testimony. God must give the reason to praise and the freedom to praise. Praise will flow naturally from lips liberated by God's salvation as surely as water flows from an uncapped artesian well.

Since praise is the theme preceding the reference to unacceptable sacrifice (v. 16), the thought here may be that the testimony of praise is the sacrifice that pleases God. Satisfying the letter of the law regarding sacrifices does not necessarily please God. Ritual rightness does not guarantee acceptance. If one's heart is not in it, if one's spirit is not right, God has no delight in mere measuring up to ritual requirements. In this the psalmist agreed with the prophets (Amos 5:21–22; Hos. 6:6; Isa. 1:10–17; Micah 6:6–8; Jer. 7:21–23).

What God requires is "a broken spirit"—not pridefulness and rebelliousness, but humbleness and submissiveness. Not only will God not "despise" such, but from man's side it is only on this basis that God is able to pardon and restore the sinner.

Prayer for Zion, 51:18–19

Zion stands for the whole congregation of God's redeemed people. Most commentators make these two verses a late addition to the psalm. The setting does seem to be after the fall of Jerusalem in 587 B.C. The Temple was destroyed, and the walls of Jerusalem were torn down. However, another interpretation is possible. Spiritual and moral implications and personal influence may be the prevailing thoughts here.

1. *To Turn Aside the Evil Effects of a Bad Example* (v. 18*a*)

Perhaps the possible effects of David's sin upon the whole nation were now the focus of thought. While it is true that sin is against God essentially, it may also adversely affect one's fellowman. Especially is this true when the sinner is a leader. The psalmist was aware that if God does good to Zion, it will be because of God's good pleasure, not the poet's good example.

2. *To Build Again What Sin Had Destroyed* (v. 18*b*)

Figuratively, Jerusalem had been reduced to ruins by David's evil deeds. "Build the walls of Jerusalem" was a request to protect Jerusalem, to be security for the people. Cities in David's day were customarily protected by massive walls. Jerusalem, the holy city, was no exception. It was David's desire that whatever harm and damage he had done through his willful sin might be repaired according to God's good pleasure to "do good to Zion." Specifically David asked the Lord to rebuild what his sin tore down.

The security of God's people has never rested in military might. History bears stark testimony to the fact that the greatest threat to any society is the enemy within. Spiritual and moral failure caused the fall of Israel, Judah, and Rome. The sin of man can tear the walls down. But only the grace of God can build the walls of security back again.

3. *To Practice Anew the Proper Balance Between Formal and Spiritual Worship* (v. 19)

The psalm closes on a note of hope that correct ritual will be matched by a contrite heart. It is the hope that out of pardon and renewal may come a right spirit and proper motive so that formal worship will again be acceptable to God. Even sin, sin in all its blackness, need not cut one off from the presence of God. Through prayer for mercy out of a contrite heart, sin can be forgiven. The barrier can be removed. Right relationships can be established. A new joy can be restored. The presence and favor of God can be assured.

When prayers seem blocked unforgiven sin may be the culprit. But the door to forgiveness is not locked. The arms of the forgiving Father are open. Even in sin a man need not be alone.

3
When Doubts Arise

Psalm 73

Problems for the righteous and prosperity for the wicked have always formed the raw products of doubt. As long as good people have it good and bad people have it bad, there is no problem. But when the righteous suffer and the wicked prosper, this blows the minds of those who must have nailed-down answers and straitjacket explanations for everything that happens to them.

The author of Job wrestled with the problem of suffering for the righteous and prosperity for the wicked. He wanted to know how to relate to God in times of calamity. Consideration of the subject led to serious doubts about the justice of God. By sermons and articles we have been urged to the conclusion that doubt is the unpardonable sin. But whatever else the book of Job teaches, it reveals that God is a friend of doubters. Job learned, and Psalm 73 underscores the lesson, that the solution to doubt is to bring the doubts into the open in the presence of God.

In Job's case, he wanted to present his case directly to God. But when God appeared and his longed-for opportunity came, he was tongue-tied. In the presence of God he did not need explanations. However, in the conclusion of the matter God justified Job for speaking openly of what was right. God honors honest doubt, but he deplores pious pretensions.

WHEN DOUBTS ARISE

The Problem Stated, 73:1-3

1. *The General Principle* (v. 1)

Verse 1 is both a confession of faith and the thesis to be debated. It is both the cause of the psalmist's doubt and the conclusion of his search. Whatever doubts Asaph, the author, had before were now settled. He was sure that "God is good to Israel" (KJV)—that is, to all of those who are "pure in heart." He was confident about God's goodness to Israel. But his experience in life "almost" cost him his faith.

Much of life gives the lie to the general principle that God is good to the pure in heart. In the face of what appears to be undeserved and meaningless suffering, the question is raised, *Why does a good God allow such?* There are observable exceptions, which sometimes create confusion.

2. *The Great Perplexity* (v. 2)

Asaph had grown uncertain about the basic truth about God's goodness. When he "saw the prosperity of the wicked" (v. 3), he almost lost his footing. His feet felt very insecure. Prosperity for the wicked didn't square with the general principle. The wicked should have suffered according to the accepted concept. Instead they prospered. Why?

3. *The Gnawing Problem* (v. 3)

Envy was eating him up! Seeing wicked men thrive had the final effect of making the writer envious of them. He wanted to have his cake and eat it too. He wanted to have his kicks from sin without suffering the kickbacks, like those arrogant and wicked men.

Envy was actually the result of looking in the wrong place. He looked at the wicked instead of God. He looked at their prosperity instead of his own treasure in God. He took a snapshot of the moment instead of a continuous movie to the explanation and contentment at the end of the reel.

The Problem Surveyed, 73:4-14

1. *Free of Problems* (vv. 4-5)

In the light of the general principle under consideration, the wicked should have suffered and the righteous should have prospered. Contrary to expectation, the psalmist observed "the prosperity of the wicked" (v. 3). He might have expressed a disinterested passion for justice. Instead he confessed to envy.

To the psalmist, the wicked seemed to be free from problems which plague other men. Their bodies are not racked with pain. To the contrary, they are "sound and sleek" (v. 4). They experience good health while other men suffer illness. Derek Kinder made this observation: "It is curious that to be physically *sound* and *sleek* is still viewed in some circles as the believer's birthright, in spite of passages such as this and, e.g., Romans 8:23; Hebrews 12:8." [1] What the poet thought he observed as he looked out upon his world was that the wicked were "not in trouble" and they were "not stricken" or plagued like other men. They seemed to be immune to sickness, sorrow, and disappointment.

As the psalmist viewed it, his world was topsy-turvy. The righteous were sick. They were plagued with trouble. In modern-day terms, they stood in the unemployment lines. They had to wrestle constantly with the dreadful dragon of inflation. They got passed by at promotion time. The wicked always seemed to have the inside track.

2. *Filled with Pride* (vv. 6-9)

As a result of the prominence their prosperity gave them, pride took possession of the wicked. But they also wore that pride like an ornament, not as a character defect. They resorted to violence in their oppression of the poor. They boasted of their pride and their violence (v. 6). Instead of hiding their misdeeds, they flaunted them.

Even their countenances were peculiarly bold because of the growth of fatty tissue around the eyes, causing the eyes to appear to stick out on stems. This caused them to look proud. Their wealth made them feel proud (v. 7b). Their words were in agreement with their appearance and attitude: "They scoff and speak with malice;/loftily they threaten oppression" (v. 8).

Prosperity brought into their lives a bumper crop of foolishness. Because they could afford it, not because there was any rhyme or reason to it, they indulged in every foolish whim their hearts could imagine. They went to the "in" places. They wore the "in" clothes. They did the "in" things. Then they flaunted it all in the face of the have-nots. Thus, they displayed their proud, arrogant attitude toward God. "Their tongue struts through the earth" (v. 9).

3. *Falsely Praised* (vv. 10–14)

"The people" points to people in general who, observing the prosperity of the wicked and the fact that they live "always at ease" (v. 12), turned to acclaim them, to approve them, and to follow them. "They" in verse 11 seems to refer to these simple people who were duped by the wicked's show of authority (vv. 8–9) and by their successful careers without interference from God. The people were so taken in by this secular approach to life that they expressed a practical atheism in the question: "How can God know?" and "Is there knowledge in the Most High?" They were not denying that there is a God. But they were asserting that he is either not aware of what's happening on earth or doesn't care.

It is no surprise that contact with wicked men who are always at ease and who increase in riches could create a tinge of envy in the heart of the righteous. The psalmist closed his description of the wicked by contrasting his own life, attitude, and success with theirs. They forgot God, stained their hands with all kinds of sins, and yet lived in luxury and ease. But the psalmist had "kept [his] heart clean" and "washed [his] hands in innocence" (v. 13). Instead of those qualities' making him immune to suffering and bringing him good health and good fortune, he experienced severe suffering "all the day long" and he was "chastened every morning" (v. 14). What should the psalmist do about this? Should he renounce his faith, peddle his doubts, or confront God and give him a chance to reclaim him?

Many renounce their faith. Who can believe in a God who runs the universe with such slipshod methods? Who can retain his faith in God when God appears to be faithless? Who can go on trusting a God who evidently favors godless men?

Many peddle their doubts. Out of personal frustration they take potshots at God, the Bible, and the church. If you get in range, they murmur and complain about the inequalities of life. They bemoan their miserable plight and blame God for mismanagement of the universe.

Our psalmist did none of these. His faith was too firmly anchored in God. The conflicting doubts only caused him to desire a confrontation with God. He was confident the conflict would clear up, if only he could present his cause directly to God.

The Problem Solved, 73:15–26

1. *Not by Public Airing of Doubts* (v. 15)

Some interpreters find the psalmist in a contradiction here. They assert that he had just said the very things he now says he will not say. Closer to the truth is that he was tempted to say this. He thought these things. But he refrained from expressing his doubts publicly for fear he might harm God's children. He dared not risk damaging the faith of one of God's little ones. Jesus warned those who would put a stumbling block in the way of God's little ones that it would be better to drown in the sea with a millstone about the neck than to offend one of his little ones (Matt. 18:6).

Perhaps the kindest gesture toward a person who publicly peddles his doubts is a terse rebuke. Somewhere I read this fitting remark for such a person: "Tell me your faith; I have doubts enough of my own." Of all the places where honesty and integrity should prevail, the pulpit should be it. But it is not a platform for peddling doubt. It is a place for preaching Christ.

2. *Not by Personal Struggle to Understand* (v. 16)

The psalmist was perplexed by what he observed. He considered voicing his doubts about the goodness and justice of God. He decided not to give public vent to his doubts lest he be a traitor among the Lord's people. The more he thought about it, the more frustrated and confused he became. The more he brooded over it, the more burdensome it became. How was he to solve his puzzling problem? Mental and rational processes alone led to weariness. Was there no answer? Where could he go? To whom could he turn?

3. *But by Presenting His Doubts to God* (vv. 17–20)

It was only after the psalmist "went into the sanctuary of God" that his doubts were resolved. This is not automatic or magical. Simply to enter the sanctuary gives no deeper insight. One must meet God there. His word must be heard, his revelation received.

Many who go to church to seek a solution to the problem of doubt come away disappointed. Sometimes the teachers or the ministers are at fault in not bringing the word of God. Often the worshiper misses the message because his antenna is not up. He's not listening. He's out of focus. He's not tuned in. There's too much "snow" and too much static.

Actually the experience described here may not be that of entering the temple at all. It may refer to an encounter with God without benefit of the temple and its ritual. Whatever the physical setting, the first step toward solution of the problem came when the psalmist focused his mind upon final issues. Worship of God adjusts the focus and enables objective evaluation.

Viewed from the present, the wicked seemed secure. Their lot in life seemed enviable. But when the psalmist "perceived their end," he realized that God had "set them in slippery places" and ultimately would "make them fall to ruin" (v. 18). They are rushing blindly and madly toward a fearful end (v. 19). Now the psalmist saw that they had no inner wealth, no genuine joys, nothing that would last. In the present, they were living in a dream world. Suddenly they would awake to reality and the phantoms of their dreams would disappear (v. 20). The long look is frequently more reliable than a snap judgment based on a single frame.

4. *By the Presence of God with the Psalmist* (vv. 21-26)

Viewing the wicked from the perspective of eternity enabled the psalmist to reevaluate his own standing with God. First, he confessed the error of his thinking and the confusion of his evaluation before going to the sanctuary, comparing himself to an embittered man and a stupid beast (vv. 21-22). Next, he expressed his newly acquired revelations through worship. Kittel calls this "The Great Nevertheless." [2] No matter what the psalmist had passed through, no matter what his doubts and fears and uncertainties— "nevertheless," he was continually with God. He was not

WHEN DOUBTS ARISE

alone. God was with him. Now he saw that he had something the wicked could never have or enjoy if they did have it. That something was the nearness of God.

The psalmist's sense of the nearness of God came not because he had clung tenaciously to God, but because God had grasped his "right hand." In the Old Testament the right hand is the symbol of power and authority. Here God grasped the psalmist's right hand. Perhaps the metaphor suggests that when man's powers are in the hand of God the greatest usefulness, harmony, and security prevail. As the psalmist saw it earlier, he was in danger of slipping. But now he saw he could not do so, for God held on to his weak child (v. 23).

Further, the psalmist asserted that God was guiding him with his counsel and afterward would "receive [him] to glory" (v. 24). Grasped by God's hand and guided by his counsel, the psalmist was sure to walk in God's ways. And afterward, he would be glorified. This may mean that he will be received into God's presence in glory. The verb "receive" is the same one used in the account of Enoch walking with God and God taking him (Gen. 5:24). This is usually interpreted to mean that Enoch went on home with God after their walk. For our purpose the question is superfluous. The language surely means he went to be with God.

It dawned upon the psalmist that he had God himself as a constant companion on earth now and the assurance of his presence throughout eternity (v. 25). What more could anyone want! Security does not depend on the strength of the follower of God, but upon the grasp, the guidance, and the goodness of God. One's "flesh" (humanness) and his "heart" (will) fail, but God will never fail. He is the psalmist's portion forever (v. 26). Human resources often are inadequate; divine resources are always abundant. Oesterley suggests that this psalmist "is certain that a material event like the dissolution of the body is powerless to break the love-forged links of the soul."[3] We might wish we could share Paul's triumphant message in Romans 8 with the psalmist. However, he had reached a station in his faith from which the doctrine of resurrection could grow. Surely he was created to walk with God and to continue in God's presence throughout eternity.

The Problem Summarized, 73:27-28

1. *Those Far Away Shall Perish* (v. 27)

The language employed here suggests sure result or startling consequences. "Lo" or "behold" always signals something significant to follow. This is an *alert* word. It says to the reader, *Pay close attention.* In this case it points to the conclusion of the whole matter.

At the beginning the psalmist was fuzzy in his thinking and frustrated in his observations. But now from the new perspective of the presence of God, he saw with clarity. Those in a truly perilous predicament are the ones who are far away from God and false in their relationships with God. The greatest wealth is the presence of God. The greatest poverty is the absence of God. The most dangerous position in one's relationship to God is distance. The greater the distance, the greater the peril! Far away from God, the wicked are sure to perish. The Hebrew word from which "perish" comes means to stray, to wander, to be lost. This is a poetic name for the netherworld. It designates the place of damnation and punishment in rabbinic literature.

"Put an end to" means to cut off or destroy. "False to thee" is literally "go awhoring from you." The wicked people's relationship to God is likened to marital infidelity. God cuts off those who go awhoring from him. What strides our psalmist had made! Once he envied the people he later pitied. Now he saw with high-noon clarity that there is a "per-

WHEN DOUBTS ARISE

ish" side to the biblical revelation. Men pass over it at their own peril. "Destruction" is the end of wickedness just as surely as "salvation" is the end of trusting God.

2. *Those Near God Have a Refuge* (v. 28)

The "good" for the psalmist was to be "near God." By implication, it was bad to be "far from" God. Distance created the problem of doubt. Closeness solved it. From that protected vantage point he vowed to share the story of his inner struggle and triumph. This is witnessing at its best.

The purpose of telling of all God's works is obviously so that other men may learn who God is and take refuge in him also. The problem which caused the psalm to be written had been solved. The simple solution to doubt is to stay near God. With that insight the psalmist was on sure ground again.

God *was* good to Israel! And he is good to all who take refuge in him. For the psalmist, making God his refuge came about through a conscious resolve. He "made" the Lord his refuge. It is the same for us all. God doesn't snatch us inside his protective care against our wills. He opens the door, but we must walk in. We must see and desire him as our refuge. The hymn writer charts the way to higher ground:

> My heart has no desire to stay
> > Where doubts arise and fears dismay;
> Tho some may dwell where these abound,
> > My prayer, my aim is higher ground.

When doubts arise, flee to God. Even in doubt, the man who trusts in God is never alone.

4
When Troubles Come

Psalm 46

Job said, "Man that is born of a woman is of few days, and full of trouble" (Job 14:1). With accusing overtones Job's friend had said, "For affliction does not come from the dust,/ nor does trouble sprout from the ground;/but man is born to trouble/as the sparks fly upward" (Job 5:6). Contrary to some popular thoughts on the subject, God's children are not immune to trouble. To live in our kind of world is to experience some kind of trouble. The amount and intensity of it will vary from person to person, family to family, and time to time. But no one escapes it altogether.

How to handle trouble is a universal problem. When troubles come some push the panic button, throw up their hands, and throw in the towel. Others moan and groan and complain. One person is trounced; the next triumphs. What makes the difference? The answer of the psalmist was simple. Some have inner reserves and resources for meeting troubles. Others do not. Those who *do* not only survive but also triumph.

The historical setting for this psalm is uncertain. Some say the Sennacherib crisis in 701 B.C. was the occasion for it. Hezekiah, king of Judah, had been "shut up like a bird in a cage" by Sennacherib, king of Assyria. It looked like sure defeat and destruction for Jerusalem. Isaiah assured the king that an arrow would not fall in Jerusalem and that

WHEN TROUBLES COME

God's presence in their midst made the city inviolable. As it turned out, Sennacherib lost 185,000 of his men in a single night and was forced to withdraw the siege and return to Assyria (Isa. 36—37).

Others connect the psalm with the wars among the successors of Alexander the Great. Yet others identify it as a hymn of the New Year's festival. Some suggest a date in Josiah's reign or in the days of Jehoshaphat (2 Chron. 20). The Sennacherib crisis referred to above probably formed the backdrop for this psalm.

Martin Luther was inspired by Psalm 46 in 1529 (when Vienna had been released from the Turkish siege) to write his great hymn "A Mighty Fortress Is Our God." As John Wesley lay dying in London, this psalm inspired his closing words: "The Lord of hosts is with us;/the God of Jacob is our refuge" (v. 11). In the fourteenth century Sergius used this psalm to inspire his men to courage in warding off the Tartar hordes. It is a psalm of triumph over trouble. Its application is wider than war and troubles related to military conquest. In my ministry God has used this psalm to still troubled hearts, to bring courage in the face of severe sickness, to restore faith in the presence of God, and to generate assurance and confidence in the sufficiency of God.

An Unassailable Refuge, 46:1–3

1. *Secure Hiding* (v. 1*a*)

Protection is one of the first needs of those who have trouble. As Leupold says, "He [God] is . . . like a strong fortress into which a man may flee and be absolutely safe." [1] What a relief it is to reach secure hiding following a close chase by a determined enemy. Usually, the last place a troubled person looks for help is God. He may run to the banker, check with his lawyer, call the police, or get an appointment with the doctor. But not many will flee to God. Since God is our refuge, "therefore, we will not fear" (v. 2)—no matter what the trouble is.

The word order of the Hebrew text makes "God" emphatic. God and nothing else is our refuge. Also, read literally, the text has "God for us refuge and strength." "For us" may suggest that he is not against us. More positively it asserts, "He is on our side." In a shout of victory Paul declared, "If God be for us, who can be against us?" (Rom. 8:31, KJV). No greater ally could be imagined.

2. *Strong Hands* (v. 1*b*)

"Strength" describes what God is to us. This means that God is on our side. No matter how strong the enemy or how fierce the trouble, God is an inexhaustible source of strength for us. Actually, the text does not say that God is the *source* of our strength. It says, "God is our strength." If he who is Master of all the powers of chaos is on our side—indeed, is our strength—we have nothing to fear. As Psalm 93 says, "The Lord reigns;/ . . . thy throne is established from of old;/ . . . /Mightier than the thunders of many waters,/mightier than the waves of the sea,/the Lord on high is mighty" (Ps. 93:1-4). And a familiar chorus says,

> He's got the whole world in his hands,
> He's got the whole world in his hands,
> He's got the whole world in his hands,
> He's got the whole world in his hands.[2]

In the Scriptures hands (especially the right hand) symbolize power and authority. In the grasp of God's strong hands, his child is secure. Speaking of the security of those who are his sheep, Jesus said, "I give them eternal life, and they shall never perish, and no man shall snatch them out of my hand. My Father, who has given them to me, is greater than all, and no one is able to snatch them out of the Father's

WHEN TROUBLES COME

hand. I and the Father are one" (John 10:28–30).

God is our strong tower, our defense, our strength. Thus, we can cope courageously with the troubles that assail us.

3. *Seasoned Helper* (v. 1c)

The second part of this verse does not stress God's presence, as the King James translators would have us understand, "a very present help in trouble." Instead, the idea is that God is a "well-proved" or seasoned helper. He has demonstrated his power, resourcefulness, and effectiveness as a helper of the troubled. He is no novice. He is well proved! Later in the psalm, God's nearness is emphasized. He is a "present," not an "absent," help in trouble. Luther's hymn asserts:

> A mighty fortress is our God,
>   A bulwark never failing;
> Our helper he, amid the flood
>   Of mortal ills prevailing.

The kind of trouble described in verses 2 and 3 is a violent earthquake. While the author had in mind physical dangers of the sort described, surely the application is wider. God is our unassailable refuge from all dangers, our defense against all enemies, our well-proved help in all circumstances.

Where I grew up in North Louisiana, storm cellars were common. Some were simple cavelike cavities in the earth. Some were more elaborate, well equipped, and well appointed. Whether plain or sophisticated, they served as a refuge from the storm. I remember hearing stories of neglect to take refuge in the cellar in the face of an approaching storm with tragic consequences. Other stories circulated of the cellar caving in because of heavy rains and suffocating an entire family. But God is our sure "refuge," our adequate "strength." He is well proved as a helper. It would be the part of wisdom to seek refuge in him.

Based on who God is as refuge, strength, and seasoned helper, the psalmist confidently concluded, "Therefore we will not fear" (v. 2). The earth might change. The mountains might shake. The seas might surge. But the psalmist would be secure. He would not fear. Only those who have gone through an earthquake can appreciate his words. Most of us have seen the earth change through erosion of its face by wind or water. An earthquake is in a different category. As Edwin McNeill Poteat suggested:

> But to feel a mountain shake and to see a crack run like a startled snake across a bare field, and to be caught in the midst of things from which one is powerless to flee—this is to know the puny strength of man when caught in the wild elemental dance of nature.[3]

Being a Christian doesn't mean there are no storms or earthquakes in your life. But it does mean you don't have to face such things alone. Being in a storm cellar doesn't alter the velocity of the wind, but it does alter the turbulence within. With Christ in the boat you need not fear.

An Unfailing Resource, 46:4–7

1. *Provision of Life* (v. 4)

The emphasis shifts from a thin and flat preservation of life to provision of a full and vibrant life. The first psalm has a similar figure. It compares a man who delights in God's teaching and meditates on his principles to a tree planted by a river. Such a tree is secure, growing, and bearing fruit.

The "river" is the "life-giving fountain of God's presence," according to William R. Taylor in *The Interpreter's Bible*.[4] Isaiah used this figure (Isa. 32:2; 33:21). Jeremiah referred to God as a "fountain of living waters" (Jer. 2:13). Ezekiel pictured God as a river bringing life wherever he flows

WHEN TROUBLES COME

(Ezek. 47:1–12). Zechariah used a similar figure of speech (Zech. 14:8). John expressed essentially the same idea when he described God's place in the New Jerusalem (Rev. 22:1–2). Not only does God's presence bring protection, safety, and help, but also life, joy, healing, and fruitfulness.

2. *Presence of the Lord* (vv. 5,7)

God "in the midst" means God is available and accessible to his people. When he is present, his people are not "moved" to fear even in the face of the fiercest enemy. *The New English Bible* reads, "God is in that city; she will not be overthrown." Later this was misunderstood to mean that never under any circumstances would the city of Jerusalem be taken by an enemy. I am convinced by history that Isaiah meant the Sennacherib crisis only. The Temple in Jerusalem was considered the "holy habitation" of God. His presence there made the city inviolable, or so it was generally believed. Any time an enemy threatened, the people believed God would "help her right early."

The darkest and most dangerous watch of the night is just before dawn. That's when one may expect God to help. A cliché of our day is "At the end of your rope? Tie a knot and hang on." But in the light of this psalm, the saying should be, "At the end of your rope? Don't worry about it! God is holding on!" Verses 7 and 11 magnify the nearness of God. "Lord of Hosts" is Isaiah's favorite name for God. "Hosts" typically refers to military forces in the earthly realm. But the term often means heavenly forces. Isaiah also had a fondness for using "Jacob" instead of "Israel" as the name for the patriarch. The same one who saw Jacob through many dangerous experiences was secure hiding for the psalmist.

Some interpreters believe the refrain in verses 7 and 11 has been left out inadvertently after verse 3. However that may be, the repetition of the refrain strongly suggests the author's intention to emphasize the potential for triumphing over trouble through the presence of God.

3. *Providence Over the Lands* (v. 6)

The first three verbs in this verse are perfects and may be rendered as that which has regularly happened. The final verb is imperfect and should be considered as descriptive of the consequences of that which regularly happens. The nations have always raged; the kingdoms have regularly tottered; but God has consistently uttered his voice in judgment. The result is that "the earth melts." That is, the earth is under the sovereign control of God. It submits to him ultimately because it must. He is in charge! How reassuring!

Yahweh, the Lord of Hosts, Israel's God now revealed in Jesus of Nazareth, is no tribal god. His realm is not some narrow strip of land in the Middle East. His authority never was limited to the motley bunch of slaves that came out of Egypt back in the thirteenth century B.C. He is the God of all the earth, the only God there is. He is sovereign ruler over all the affairs of men. This is comforting when an aggressive nation sets out upon a campaign to conquer the world. Amid tottering kingdoms (our own is shaky at times), it is reassuring to remember the assertion of this psalmist. When God utters his voice, that settles it. The earth submits.

An Unbeatable Rescuer, 46:9-11

1. *Desolation of the Enemy* (v. 9)

Charred chariots, broken bows, shattered spears, and dead bodies are the visible evidence of God's wrath upon the psalmist's enemies. He has in view a present picture, a current crisis. This, as we have already indicated, was probably the Sennacherib threat against Jerusalem in 701 B.C., when the Assyrian army was turned back by the timely intervention of God. Mysteriously and miraculously 185,000 Assyrian soldiers died in a night. It was clear to all that Judah's God had delivered Hezekiah with a dazzling demonstration.

Those who came out of Egyptian bondage by the mighty hand of God were commanded to tell the story to every succeeding generation. Men tend to forget the marvelous interventions of God. The psalmist invited beleaguered followers of God to look upon God's work. We are forced to look at what the devil has done via television, newspapers, and other public media. Lest we forget what God has done, let us look again and again to a rugged hill called Calvary. Also, there are an empty tomb, a militant church, and transformed lives.

2. *Destruction of War Implements* (v. 9)

In the Sennacherib incident a war had been made to cease. There was no doubt in anyone's mind as to who did it. Men have demonstrated the ability to make war throughout the generations. In this crisis God demonstrated the ability to make war to cease. The ultimate victory of the Lord must have encouraged the besieged people of Jerusalem.

Isaiah (2:4) and Micah (4:3-4) picture a warless world on the heels of the establishment of the kingdom of God. These prophets predicted a transformation of war implements into farm implements. The psalmist described the destruction of war implements. The result in all cases is peace. We are keenly aware that men are still capable of making war. We need to be reminded that God is still capable of making peace. And it doesn't matter whether the problem is a civil war inside a man, a domestic wrangle inside the family, or an atomic holocaust involving this entire globe.

3. *Deliverance of Those Who "Know" God* (v. 10)

Verse 10 is addressed to all those forces in the universe

opposed to God. "To be still" is to desist, to refrain, to relax. It is an imperative. God's enemies are commanded to cease from what they are doing, to put a stop to their rebellious actions, to let the reins of their lives fall into the hands of God. "Know" means intimate, experiential knowledge. It means to know unquestionably God's presence, help, and blessing. The command calls upon the nations to realize what it means to have God in their midst. To "exalt" him as God means their deliverance.

Only those who "know" God in this way can be assured of his salvation. He is an unbeatable rescuer. He deals with our enemies, destroys their implements of war, and delivers those who know him. With God in our midst we should never fear. But, trusting him, we should triumph over all trouble. When troubles come it helps to remember that you are not alone.

5
When Sickness Strikes

Psalm 6

In the psalmist's day it was generally believed that affliction of whatever kind was an expression of God's ill will and displeasure. Unlike Job, the psalmist did not plead innocence. Unlike other psalmists, he did not cry for vengeance upon his enemies. The pains and sufferings of the psalmist were likened to the blows of a rod in the hands of an angry God.

The fact of his suffering, intense suffering, is quite clear. The cause of his suffering is not as clear. It may have been physical suffering, stemming from physical illness. Or it may have been mental and emotional suffering, knowing the nature of his sin. Or it may have been the suffering of a physical ailment caused by a spiritual problem. Or it may have been mental and spiritual suffering caused by a physical malady. Part of the suffering was caused by the apparent delight his contemporaries took in awaiting the outcome of his affliction.

Modern medical technology has demonstrated the connection between the mind and the body in sickness. Psychosomatic medicine has become an effective procedure for treating certain physical and organic malfunctions. This approach takes into account the fact that the mind may cause some sicknesses involving organic disorders. In more recent times the medical profession has come to recognize yet another dimension to illness. Some sickness is caused by spiritual problems. Just as mental and emotional illness may adversely affect physical functions, so spiritual illness may produce both mental and physical problems.

A physician connected with the medical school in Galveston, Texas, asked me to work with him in treating a member of the congregation I served in Alvin, Texas. He suspected that beyond the patient's physical and emotional illness lay some unresolved spiritual problems. Poor spiritual health can lead to mental illness and result in physical malfunctions. Man's makeup reflects a rather precarious balance. So when a person is out of balance in his relationship to God, this may lead to a mental or physical imbalance.

Serious sickness is a shattering experience to many people, especially those who have enjoyed uninterrupted good health throughout life. Some are so fearful of fatal illness that they call the doctor every time they sneeze. Others are afraid to call the doctor even in the face of extreme symptoms, for fear they may have some dread disease. William R. Taylor describes the extremity of the psalmist's illness when he says, "So great is his distress that his death seems close at hand (v. 5)." [1]

Three stack poles around which we will gather the psalmist's thoughts are: (1) sin, (2) suffering, and (3) salvation.

Sin, 6:1–5

1. *The Cause of Affliction* (v. 1)

Though sin is nowhere mentioned in the psalm, it is everywhere implicit. The Lord's rebuke in anger and chastening in wrath implies sin in the psalmist. Some interpreters have supposed that the poet's plea is for love-rebuke instead of anger-rebuke from God. What the author sought, according to this view, was correction in love. But in the context it seems more likely that the psalmist was asking for the removal of correction altogether, since correction from any motivation suggests the anger of God. The prayer of the psalmist acknowledged that he had fallen out of the favor of God and was a petition for reinstatement. Leupold asserts that this is "the equivalent of a free and full confession of sin and utter unworthiness." [2]

"Rebuke" suggests that wrong has been done. It is an acknowledgment of sin and the appropriateness of rebuke. The wrong should not have been done. "Chasten" describes positive action to put right the person in question. Chastisement implies a redemptive purpose. It is not to be understood as God's gleeful administration of a spanking to his child. It is meant to help. When parents spank their children, they often say, "It hurts me more than it hurts you" or "I'm doing this for your good." Children don't believe that statement at the time; when they are parents they may. The disposition to begin the search for God's purpose in illness is the turning point in the disease. Whether one's health is restored or not, looking for the good God wants one to get out of sickness is the turning point.

"Wrath" is stronger than "anger." It means "hot displeasure." Never is it to be equated with man's uncontrolled temper tantrums. It is the utter revulsion of God's nature against sin. And this in no way prohibits his loving the very sinner whose sin provokes his wrath. So here is a plea for forgiveness and an admission that the wrong done is so serious that it must be disposed of. Forgiveness is the only way to dispose of it.

2. *The Cry for Mercy* (v. 2*a*)

The appeal to put an end to the pain of rebuke and chastening is not based on merit. Any thought of merit is ruled out by the plea "Be gracious to me" (RSV) or "Have mercy upon me" (KJV). Thus, the psalmist understood the gospel of grace. Like the poor sinner in Jesus' story, the psalmist pled mercy, not merit.

"Languishing" is from a word meaning to be sick, to droop, or to waste away. The psalmist seemed to expect God to be touched by his frailty. Psalm 103 puts it this way: "For he knows our frame;/he remembers that we are dust" (v. 14). The Creator cannot forget the stuff of which the creature is made. He knows that our feet are made of clay. He understands us. He knows our weaknesses. He is merciful. The hymn writer understood the psalmist, for he wrote:

> I am weak but thou art strong;
> > Jesus, keep me from all wrong;
> I'll be satisfied as long
> > As I walk, let me walk close to thee.

3. *The Call for Healing* (v. 2*b*)

"Heal me" may have a broader application than physical healing. It may include every "restorative work that God does upon body and soul." [3] The keenness of pain over sin is described as a terror felt in the bones. "Troubled" means terrified, or paralyzed with fear. Some may take sin lightly. The psalmist trembled with fear.

Therefore, the basis of the psalmist's appeal for mercy was not only his weakness but also his terror. His bones were troubled, and his soul was sorely troubled. Paralyzing fear was what the psalmist experienced. What a dreadful thing sin is! It is not to be taken lightly or laughed out of the court of consideration as though it is of no consequence. Sin is serious. Sickness is shattering. Fear is paralyzing. God's wrath is awesome.

A sick person wants one thing—to get well. Asking the Lord to heal him revealed the psalmist's conviction that the Lord has the power to do it. Further, it is testimony of his faith in the Great Physician. A large segment of Christianity deplores the use of doctors, medicines, and medical technology in treating illness. In my judgment, the psalmist was not arguing that question. He was acknowledging the ultimate source of all healing—with or without, or even in spite of—medicines, doctors, and technology.

4. *The Complaint Against God* (v. 3)

"Soul" is "life," and it is an advance over the previous statement. First the psalmist's bones were troubled. Now his soul was sorely troubled. His whole life was paralyzed by fear. Adding to his distress was the absence of God. "But thou, O Lord—how long?" The thought may be, *How long will you remain inactive? It's time for you to do something.* Or the thought may be, *How long must I suffer? I can't stand any more pain.*

Psalm 13 has these additional insights into the meaning of the question "How long?" "How long . . . Wilt thou forget me for ever? . . . wilt thou hide thy face from me, . . . must I bear pain in my soul, . . . shall my enemy be exalted over me?" (vv. 1–2). Had the psalmist dropped out of the favor of God? Was God responsible for the psalmist's sickness? Was God on the side of the psalmist's enemies?

Based on the next thought presented by the psalmist, his dominant feeling here may have been that God had abandoned him. He was complaining that in the time when he needed God most, God was absent! How different is the testimony of the hymn writer:

> Just when I need him,
>   Jesus is near,
> Just when I falter,
>   just when I fear;
> Ready to help me,
>   ready to cheer,
> Just when I need him most.

5. *The Command to Save* (v. 4)

"Turn" may mean return, or even repent. It is the word regularly used to describe repentance. When used of God it is often an appeal for God to change his announced judgment. Here it may refer to what the psalmist saw as God's purpose through his illness. So the plea was, "Don't let me die. Let me live."

"Turn," "save," and "deliver me" are all imperatives. While it may seem strange to us for men ever to command God to do anything, the psalmist knew that God is pleased to do what he purposes for man's best interests. Notice that the psalmist based his command to save on God's "steadfast love," not on his merit. This is often called covenant love. It declares God's commitment to act always in the best interests of his people.

"Life" (RSV) is rendered "soul" in the King James Version. It is from *nephesh*. "Life" is probably the better translation; but the reference may include spiritual salvation as well as physical deliverance. It means "make me well and make me whole."

6. *The Concern About Praise* (v. 5)

Reference to death here confirms the fact that the psalmist expected his illness to result in death. The poet did not deny any good in the hereafter. However, he does seem to have lost sight of whatever revelation was available to God's people in his day concerning the afterlife. Death appeared to the psalmist as such a shadowy existence "that he feels he would not be able there to remember God's goodness and praise Him for it." [4] Part of his appeal to God to save him was based on his conviction that descent into death would eliminate any possibility of praise there. God would be minus one voice of praise.

To appreciate the fuller revelation to Old Testament fol-

WHEN SICKNESS STRIKES 67

lowers of God, one should study Job 19:25–27; Psalm 16:8–11; Isaiah 26:19; and Daniel 12:2–3. But when a man is sick and death stares him in the face, fear may blind his faith and paralyze his hope. The positive side of this negative statement about death (no remembrance of God in Sheol, no opportunity to praise God there) is the recognition that God delights in the praise of his children. Praising is better than thanking. Praising God exalts him.

Suffering, 6:6–7

1. *Weariness* (v. 6 *a*)

The results of sin are expressed in terms of weariness, weeping, and weakness. The psalmist had worn himself out with his sighings. Nothing is more taxing than physical pain, emotional stress, and spiritual agony. This explains the washed-out feeling following a season of prolonged stress. Suffering for a short time is bearable by most everyone. But suffering stretched over many days, weeks, months, and years can be overwhelming.

In the prologue to the book of Job, the author pictured Job's first response to calamity: "Then Job arose, and rent his robe, and shaved his head, and fell upon the ground, and worshiped. And he said, 'Naked I came from my mother's womb, and naked shall I return; the Lord gave, and the Lord has taken away; blessed be the name of the Lord'" (Job 1:20–21).

What a beautiful example of piety, resignation, and submission to God! But that wasn't the end of the story. Satan afflicted Job with loathsome sores. His friends came to comfort him. For seven days they sat in silence (the period of mourning for the dead), so disfigured and pitiful was Job. Now he is not portrayed as such a fine model of patience and piety.

When Job opened his mouth this time, he "cursed" (not

"blessed") the day of his birth. What made the difference? At least part of the explanation must be that he had grown weary with unending pain and suffering day after day.

2. *Weeping* (vv. 6b–7a)

By use of a hyperbole, the psalmist said he flooded his bed with tears every night. His may have been the original waterbed, soaked with the tears of bitter, unrelenting grief. The next morning his eyes were swollen and worn out with weeping and want of sleep. Lasting grief had caused his eye to lose its luster.

Another psalmist bravely submitted, "Weeping may endure for a night, but joy cometh in the morning" (30:5, KJV). But our psalmist claimed that "every night" he flooded his bed with tears. His pain was persistent. He appears to have been on a merry-go-round with no end to his suffering. He was in a dark tunnel and he saw no light at the end of it. Like Job, he "pours out tears to God" (Job 16:20).

3. *Weakness* (v. 7b)

"Weak" in the Revised Standard Version refers to the eye. The grief the psalmist's foes have caused him had made him weak and old. The eyes swell and appear weak after extended periods of grief and weeping. Instead of "foe" (RSV), I prefer "distresses" (with the Septuagint). This seems to fit the context better. Anyone who has endured long tenures of suffering usually shows it by appearing to be older than he is. The eyes especially are apt to show the signs of prolonged suffering.

In the aftermath of illness, often the patient is left with a feeling of weakness and impotency. Isaiah's word has been a source of strength for many: "Have you not known? Have you not heard? The Lord is the everlasting God,/the Creator of the ends of the earth./He does not faint or grow weary,/

WHEN SICKNESS STRIKES

his understanding is unsearchable./He gives power to the faint,/and to him who has no might he increases strength./ Even youths shall faint and be weary,/and young men shall fall exhausted;/but they who wait for the Lord shall renew their strength,/they shall mount up with wings like eagles,/ they shall run and not be weary,/they shall walk and not faint" (Isa. 40:28-31).

Sometimes it seems that until a man is flat on his back with illness, he will not look up to God at all. In Job's case, he admitted a kind of secondhand knowledge of God. But he had his eyes opened through suffering. He stated it this way: "I had heard of thee by the hearing of the ear,/but now my eye sees thee" (Job 42:5). Stephen had a similar experience. Facing the Sanhedrin, who were enraged by his words, Stephen "gazed into heaven and saw the glory of God, and Jesus standing at the right hand of God" (Acts 7:55). Then Stephen was stoned to death with his heart serene in the assurance that Jesus was ready to receive him into heaven and with a prayer on his lips for his executioners.

Salvation, 6:8-10

1. *Assurance* (v. 8)

The assurance of forgiveness, recovery, and salvation is explained in a bold command to the poet's enemies: "Depart from me, all you workers of evil" (v. 8*a*). The ground of assurance was the psalmist's confidence that the Lord had heard his weeping. It is not difficult for Christians to identify with this sharp change in mood. Here is one like us who had gone into the presence of God with his particular trouble and had freely unburdened his heart. He had been greatly comforted by having confessed his sin and having deposited his burden with God.

The psalmist believed that God was touched by his tears. At least he was persuaded that God heard the sound of his weeping. At one point in his grief he felt forsaken by God (6:4). Now he was assured that God was near enough to hear his crying.

2. *Acceptance* (v. 9)

Not only had the Lord heard the sound of the psalmist's weeping, but also he had heard his "supplication." The Hebrew word is usually rendered "entreaty." Some commentators translate "plea for mercy." This opened a window into the psalmist's house of tears. He was not merely indulging in self-pity. Through the salty bitterness of his tears, he got hold of the horns of the altar of God. He was not simply pitying himself; he was pleading for mercy.

Aware that the Lord had heard his entreaty, he was assured that God would now accept his prayer or receive his messages again. Earlier he had felt exiled from God. Now the lines of communication were opened again. It is not unusual that at the conclusion of a bout with serious illness there comes a fresh assurance of acceptance with God and the closeness of God.

3. *Ashamed* (v. 10)

The closing thought expressed the psalmist's certainty that all his enemies would be put to shame. The terror and paralyzing fear that they had observed in him would now fall on them. This, he was sure, would come "in a moment." The shame of his enemies was an additional statement of the psalmist's assurance. Perhaps, like Job's friends, they had accused him of secret sins as the explanation for his sickness. They were the real "workers of evil," and now they would be "sorely troubled" as proof of it. In the writer's mind this would result in a more secure standing with God for him.

Surely there is a tie between sin and sickness and suffering. But it is not good for us to see someone in great suffering and automatically conclude that the person is a great sinner. Jesus suffered greatly, but one would hardly conclude from that fact that he was a great sinner.

The prophet predicted a vicarious suffering (suffering in our behalf) for one called "my servant." Look at his testimony: "Surely he has borne our griefs/and carried our sorrows;/yet we esteemed him stricken,/smitten by God, and afflicted./But he was wounded for our transgressions,/he was bruised for our iniquities;/upon him was the chastisement that made us whole,/and with his stripes we are healed" (Isa. 53:4–5).

Healing and health and wholeness are in God's hands.

6
When Fears Dismay

Psalm 27

Theodore Roosevelt said, "The only thing we have to fear is fear itself." That may be true. But few people go through life without experiencing paralyzing, bone-rattling, and sometimes crippling fear. Children learn very early to fear the dark. It is natural and healthy to fear the unknown. However, many of our most destructive fears are completely unfounded, unhealthy, and unnatural.

Some people have an unnatural fear of thunderstorms. I have known people to fear high places or closed places. Some people fear disease. Others fear doctors. Yet others fear failure. In the Gentilly area where I live in New Orleans, many parents fear for the lives of their children because of recent deaths by indiscriminate sniper fire.

The psalmist was dealing with the problem of fear. This psalm tells us how to have freedom from fear. Actually, what the psalmist discovered through experience was that God does not always remove the source of fear. But he does give inward resources to deal with fear. The essence of the idea is the presence of God. The author of Hebrews sounded a similar note: "For he hath said, I will never leave thee, nor forsake thee. So that we may boldly say, The Lord is my helper, and I will not fear what man shall do unto me" (Heb. 13:5–6). If we can but know that we do not face the fearful circumstances alone, we tend to be calmer.

WHEN FEARS DISMAY

When a child is walking in the dark, his fears quickly subside if only the warm, strong hand of a parent is offered. The embrace of a friend can steady the nerves and calm the spirit of one who has just learned of the tragic death of a loved one. In the face of the doctor's announcement of the need for radical surgery, a church member receives comfort and strength from the presence and ministry of the pastor. If divorce causes a woman's world to come crashing down around her, the attendant fears may be dispelled by a friend who has been in the same situation and who is willing to listen with empathy. The presence of one other person in a fearful situation will go a long way toward dealing with the fears involved. Especially is this true when the other person and presence is none other than God the Almighty himself.

Most interpreters have concluded that Psalm 27 is composed of what was originally two separate psalms: (1) a song of trust, verses 1–6, and (2) a plea for help, verses 7–14. In the first section, it would seem that the trust of the psalmist developed out of experience. He had faced adversaries, foes, and many days of trouble. Otherwise, how could he have known that the Lord was light, salvation, and a stronghold? In the second section, the psalmist cried out for help to the God he had already learned to trust through previous days of troubles.

I see no necessity for assigning the psalm to two authors or to two separate periods by one author. Religious experience frequently fluctuates in mood. We will treat the psalm as a unit. Perhaps the point the author makes by joining these two conflicting moods together is that in the midst of trouble, first concentrate upon the changeless Helper. Then face the fearful trouble, pleading for courage and help from the God who has proved to be the greatest helper that humans could ever have.

Confidence in God, 27:1-6

1. *His Protection* (vv. 1-3)

The confidence of the psalmist was based on who God is—light, salvation, stronghold—in relationship to the psalmist. Notice the assertion that the Lord is "my" light, "my" salvation, and the stronghold of "my" life. This is a declaration of the psalmist's personal faith. Since men fear the dark, the need is for light. When men are caught in the clutches of evil, the need is for deliverance. If men are assailed by their enemies, the need is for a stronghold. God was all of this to the psalmist. This strong declaration was based on previous experience in which God proved to be these things.

"Light" means joy (Ps. 97:11), prosperity (Job 29:3), and life (Ps. 36:9). Frequently, in the Old Testament as well as the New, light means revelation. To walk in the light is to be guided by the revealed will and purpose of God. "Salvation" means rescue, deliverance, or spiritual salvation. In this context, the emphasis is probably on physical deliverance. "Stronghold" is a refuge into which one may flee for protection in time of danger. The idea of protection and deliverance is carried through verses 2 and 3.

"Evildoers" who are identified as the psalmist's "adversaries" were made to stumble and fall because God was at hand. Reference may be to the opposition party at the time of Absalom's revolt. "Eat up my flesh" (KJV) in the Aramaic means "slander," as Daniel 3:8 and 6:24 demonstrate. An individual, an army, or a whole war cannot shake the confidence the psalmist had in the protective care of God. Thus, protected with such complete care, the heart was confident.

What produces fear? Sometimes it is the uncertainty of the unknown. Sometimes it is the certainty of the known. Fear and anxiety are different things altogether. Anxiety usually exists without a definite cause. Fear usually is founded in facts. But that's good. Facts can be faced. Phantoms, to the contrary, are as slippery as eels. Facing fears may not erase them. But, once understood, they may be endured courageously. The psalmist had discovered that it is possible to deal with fears. The light of God may dispel their scary shadows. His salvation may set one free from the shackling, paralyzing results of fear. More than that, one who is afraid may flee to God as a refuge against that which strikes fear in the heart. The psalmist considered all this and concluded that there was no one and nothing which should cause him to be afraid.

What is your fear? Death, disease, failure, being alone, retirement, unemployment, living longer than your mate? The list could be extended almost without limits, so numerous are the fears of this age. Once Jesus' disciples feared a storm. After the Lord spoke the storm into a calm, he asked his disciples about their faith. Perhaps he meant what the psalmist had learned about God being light, salvation, and a stronghold. By confident trust God had entered the fearful scene and the psalmist's fears were gone. With God present, why should he fear? Jesus was saying, "Trust me. I am with you in the boat. You should have been able to control your fears."

Isaiah declared, "Behold, God is my salvation; I will trust and not be afraid" (Isa. 12:2, KJV). When the Egyptian chariots were bearing down upon the Israelites trapped between Pharaoh's forces and the sea, the writer reported about Israel, "They were in great fear" (Ex. 14:10). Moses counseled them, "Fear not [they had been fearing], stand firm [they had been wavering], and see the salvation of the Lord [they had seen only the marching Egyptians]" (Ex. 14:13).

Later, when God came down to meet the liberated Israelite slaves, the author of Exodus said that "the people were afraid and trembled" (Ex. 20:18). Moses calmed them and instructed them, "Do not fear; for God has come to prove you [prove by testing], and that the fear of him [not a quaking, trembling fear, but a reverent awe] may be before your eyes, that you may not sin" (Ex. 20:20). There is an unhealthy fear that leads to quaking and trembling. But there is a healthy respect for God which leads to putting away sin.

2. *His Presence* (v. 4)

The one thing the psalmist requested of the Lord and the one thing he vowed to seek after was the real presence of God. To "dwell in the house of the Lord all the days of my life" probably does not refer to the temple at Jerusalem—at least not literally living there for the rest of life. Rather, the thought is living in perpetual fellowship with God.

Jacob lay down alone to rest from his flight from Esau, only to discover that the flat rock on which he placed his head was "the house of God." He had a vision of God there. He worshiped God there. That was God's house for Jacob. He was not alone. Some days we may feel lonely. But we can know the uninterrupted presence of God every day and in every way that we take. The author of Proverbs exhorted, "In all your ways acknowledge him,/and he will make straight your paths" (Prov. 3:6).

To look upon "the beauty of the Lord" is interpreted by some to mean all the appointments of the temple which gave the psalmist a sense of the presence of God (Ps. 90:17; 135:3). The term translated "beauty" means pleasantness, graciousness, beauty. It pictures one living under the grace, mercy, and favor of the Lord. We sing,

> Turn your eyes upon Jesus,
>   Look full in his wonderful face,
> And the things of earth will grow strangely dim
>   In the light of his glory and grace.

WHEN FEARS DISMAY

Facing Jesus will go a long way toward preparing us to face our fears. A little time spent in looking upon the beauty of the Lord takes a lot of the ugliness out of life.

Two different words are used for God's dwelling place prior to settlement of Israel in the land of promise. One is "booth," recalling the protection God's presence brought to the wilderness wanderers. The other is "tabernacle," referring to the temporary, traveling presence of God before the Temple was built in Jerusalem. But the word used here is the word for palace or temple. It was looked upon as the place of the real presence of God. To "inquire" is to search or to ask guidance from the Lord in all the situations of existence. Thus, to "dwell" in the house of the Lord, to "behold" the beauty of the Lord, and to "inquire" in his temple all speak of the real presence, the ready accessibility of the Lord. It must have been by going to church and participating in corporate worship that the psalmist's faith was renewed and his hope inspired.

3. *His Provision* (v. 5)

Growing out of such close fellowship with God would come certain benefits to the psalmist. He would be sheltered in the day of trouble until the danger was passed. Going to church was not done to escape the trouble of the world. Rather, it was to be equipped to meet the trouble that was sure to come. As a hen hovers over her chicks when a hawk approaches, so God shelters his people until the threat (for which they are not prepared) has passed.

The psalmist was confident that he would be concealed under the cover of God's tent as a child of the heavenly Father. To be under the canopy of God's care, protection, and provision is to amass resources for meeting trouble victoriously. The Lord would set the psalmist high upon a rock out of the reach of the enemy. He would provide the protection the psalmist needed from fear and the revenge of the enemy.

4. *The Psalmist's Promise* (v. 6)

Victory over one's enemies results from staying close to God. The psalmist would come through the assaults of his enemies confident and safe in the keeping of the Lord. He promised to "offer . . ./sacrifices with shouts of joy" and add his personal songs and music in praise of the Lord. Thus, the psalmist would acknowledge the source of his strength and the real victor in his battle with fear. Freedom from fear is often to be found in a confident faith in God.

Conquest Through Prayer, 27:7-14

1. *Expecting God's Answer* (v. 7)

The confidence of the first part of the poem is missing and an anxious plea dominates this portion. The poet cried out to the Lord, "Hear . . . ,/be gracious . . . and answer me!" These are urgent, imperative appeals. He had "lost his assurance of being heard and helped. But faith is not prostrate; he still knows that God can be appealed to." [1] For that reason he commanded God to hear, to be gracious, and to answer him. The very uttering of prayer implies expectation of an answer. While confidence was gone, the road to conquest was still open.

Victory does not depend on my assurance. It depends on God's presence to act in my behalf. The psalmist's request for mercy was a confession of guilt feelings. Before he could deal with his adversaries, he had to be sure of his standing with God. Through prayer, request was made and God's answer was assured.

Frequently God's answers to our prayers are missed because we don't wait around for them. We are in far too big a hurry to wait. Most of us have so streamlined life that we must have instant everything, lest we miss something terribly important. Much of the Bible bears witness to the value of waiting. The psalmist could calmly declare, "For thee [God] I wait all the day long" (Ps. 25:5). Can you imagine having to wait all day on anything or anybody, even God? Most of us fuss and fume if we have to wait five extra minutes in the checkout line at a store. Another psalmist asserted, "Our eyes wait upon the Lord our God, until that he have mercy upon us" (123:2, KJV). Expectancy is in the wait and, with it, an air of excitement may be picked up in the words.

Isaiah pictured a patient God waiting on us so that he may be gracious to us. But only those who wait for him will be blessed. Look at his testimony: "Therefore the Lord waits to be gracious to you;/. . ./blessed are all those who wait for him" (Isa. 30:18). The book of Lamentations has this nugget: "The Lord is good to those who wait for him,/ to the soul that seeks him./It is good that one should wait quietly/for the salvation of the Lord" (Lam. 3:25–26). Jesus taught us to ask, believing. Faith means we are trusting him to answer.

2. *Obeying God's Instruction* (v. 8)

God's instruction was clear: "Seek ye my face," which means "seek my presence." This in turn implies, "Seek my favor." The poet's response was and would continue to be constant. "Thy face, Lord, do I seek." Leupold suggests this paraphrase: "Of thee my mind has always thought; my face has always sought thee; Thy face, O Lord, I will continue to seek." [2] The point is the psalmist had been obedient to follow the Lord's instruction and to seek his presence.

The poet was encouraged to pray to God though he had a deep sense of sin and guilt which had separated him from fellowship with God. Like a flash of light in the dark, he remembered a command of God, "Seek ye my face." But veiled in the command is a promise. He was willing to obey the command because he understood the promise. He saw that the very command "Seek ye my face" was an invitation and an offer. If the Lord commands us to seek, it must be possible to find his face and to be restored to his favor. It must mean that God is ready to be gracious to us the moment we begin to seek. Jeremiah spoke for God: "You will seek me and find me; when you seek me with all your heart, I will be found of you, says the Lord" (Jer. 29:13-14). And our Lord encouraged, "Seek, and you will find" (Matt. 7:7). His blessings and the fulfillment of his promises wait upon our faithfulness to obey. How often we cut ourselves off from God's riches because we don't ask for them!

3. *Requesting God's Accessibility* (vv. 9-10)

Durham says of the psalmist, "His confidence in the benefits of Yahweh's Presence is firm, but he is anxious, in his need, fearing that this Presence may be inaccessible to him in some way." [3] He was anxious lest God hide from him or turn him away. In the past the poet had known God's help, but he feared being cast off and forsaken by the Lord. Thus, he prayed that God would not hide his face or turn him aside, cast him off, or forsake him.

Taylor interprets the statement "For my father and my mother have forsaken me" to mean that "all his kith and kin, his natural allies, have denied him help." [4] This could be a reference to the time when David found it necessary to take his parents to Moab to be left in the king's care (1 Sam. 22:3-4). If so, the word rendered "forsake" may be a bit strong. The idea would be that they left him, all right; but there is no criticism of them for it. They had to leave. It was David's idea that they leave. The sense of the verse would be that when all earthly help fails, God can be counted upon for help. God will never fail to help anyone who prays

WHEN FEARS DISMAY

with the right spirit. God plus one is a majority.

4. *Asking for God's Way* (v. 11)

The request reflects openness to be taught and willingness to be led. Apparently the Lord's way was thought to be trouble free. However, many pilgrims have not found it so. A "level path" would suggest a way "calculated to miss the ambushes of those who lie in wait for him." [5] It would be a path minus large rocks behind which an enemy might lurk for the purpose of waylaying an unsuspecting traveler. At least the psalmist was expressing his faith that into whatever kinds of roads or valleys the Lord might lead him, that same Lord would meet his every need and keep him from falling into the hands of his enemies.

The verb translated "teach" has the basic root idea of to cast, to throw, or to shoot. In the form of the verb found here, it means to point out, to show, to instruct, or to teach. Isaiah reminds us, "All we like sheep have gone astray;/ we have turned every one to his own way" (Isa. 53:6). Later, men were exhorted by Isaiah (as he spoke for God): "Seek the Lord while he may be found,/call upon him while he is near;/let the wicked forsake his way" (Isa. 55:6–7). Why should the wicked forsake his way? It is because God's ways are higher (Isa. 55:9) and they lead to better things.

5. *Seeking God's Protection* (v. 12)

What the poet asked now was not to be handed over to his enemies. "Will" is from *nephesh,* usually translated "soul"; but it probably means "desire" here. "Violence" means that the psalmist's life was in danger. Thus, his need was for protection from those who "breathe out violence."

This request of the psalmist betrays a conviction of his heart. He had felt secure in God's protective care. But now he felt threatened by his enemies. Like a deer pursued with a steady bark by a persistent hound, the psalmist felt his enemies pressing upon them. They were employing devious and threatening methods. Though it is not stated, the false witnesses must have been secured by the poet's adversaries. In addition to that, scare tactics were being used: "They breathe out violence."

It was only after the psalmist had begun to secure his own relationship to God that he ventured the request for protection from the lies, slander, and violence of his enemies. Artur Weiser offers this insight: "Only those who have surrendered their hearts to the will of God in humility and are ready to act according to that will avoid the risk of seeking to make God the servant of their own desires in asking for external help." [6] The psalmist's openness to be taught God's way and his willingness to be led in God's path put him in a position not only to ask God's protection from his enemies, without self-righteous arrogance, but also to expect God's favorable answer.

6. *Anticipating God's Goodness* (v. 13)

The incompleteness of this verse is hidden in many of the translations. The Revised Standard Version has "I believe that I shall see the goodness of the Lord/in the land of the living." But a literal rendering reflects the abrupt interruption of the flow of thought: "Unless I had believed to see the goodness of the Lord in the land of the living____!" The very incompleteness of the sentence is a strong declaration of the poet's faith. The implication of the silence could be something like this: "Unless I had believed to see the goodness of the Lord in the land of the living, I would have utterly lost heart and hope." But the break off of the thought leaves a positive affirmation. "I did believe. I expected to experience the goodness and the grace of God in the midst of the threats of my enemies." This was no

WHEN FEARS DISMAY

"pie in the sky by and by" proof which he anticipated. So confident was he that the object of his faith was already on its way that he resolved to wait for it.

The King James Version has an addition to the text: "I had fainted, unless I had believed to see the goodness of the Lord in the land of the living." "I had fainted" is helpful, but limiting. It is stronger simply to have the sentence break off. His faith strongly anticipates the evidences of God's favor. "In the land of the living" means "in this life." This verse represents a sharp turn in mood back to the confidence of the first part of the poem. The sunshine of his faith had begun to break up the clouds of his fear.

7. *Awaiting God's Response* (v. 14)

Those who want to make this a temple experience explain the last verse as the response of the temple priest to the psalmist's prayer. However, I favor the interpretation of Durham, who makes this verse the psalmist's words "half to himself and half to any who will listen." [7] Thus, the poet was confident that he would experience the delivering presence of God as he had so earnestly requested. We, too, can be "more than conquerors through him who loved us" (Rom. 8:37). Fear fades in the face of faith in the Lord.

Israel was in exile in Babylon, cut off from the holy city of Jerusalem, denied worship in the familiar setting of the Temple, discouraged about their future as a people, and feeling forsaken by God. Ah, but good tidings are on the way: "Behold the Lord comes with might,/and his arm rules for him;/behold his reward is with him,/and his recompense before him./He will feed his flock like a shepherd,/he will gather the lambs in his arms,/he will carry them in his bosom,/and gently lead those that are with young" (Isa. 40:10–11).

Though they felt that their way was hidden from the Lord

(Isa. 40:27) and that all the music had gone out of life (Ps. 137:2-4), the never-faint, never-weary God gives power to the faint; and to him who has no might he increases strength (Isa. 40:29). But this blessing is reserved for those only who are patient enough to wait for it. What a cheering note indeed for all who are faint with fear is this word from the psalmist: "Wait for the Lord;/be strong and let your heart take courage;/yea, wait for the Lord" (27:14).

When fears dismay and dishearten God's children, how good it is to be strengthened by the inner reserves deposited by faith. Waiting seems such a silly waste to some. But waiting which steels the inner person against stresses of outer pressures is a good stewardship of time.

7
When Guilt Overwhelms

Psalm 32

This is the second of seven penitential psalms in the Psalter (Pss. 6,32,38,51,102,130,143). These are recited or sung by many Christians in the Lenten season. Psalm 32 is from the Davidic collection and has been understood traditionally as related to David's sin with Bathsheba (2 Sam. 11). The superscription refers to the psalm as a Maskil, a didactic poem. Certainly the psalm contains a valuable insight about how to deal with sin.

From Adam and Eve to the present, the natural tendency has been to conceal sin or to hide the sinner. That approach didn't work for Adam and Eve, and it doesn't work for us. We cannot follow the "ignore it and it will go away" philosophy. Another approach that Adam and Even took, one which we often take, is to rationalize our sin. Given the circumstances of a luscious fruit and a subtle serpent, sin is unavoidable, we conclude. But as someone has rightly observed, "The problem was not the apple on the tree, but the *pair* on the ground."

Another tack we take is to blame somebody else. We pass the buck as Adam and Eve did. We say that it was that woman or that serpent. Yet another tendency we have in dealing with sin is to hide the sinner. Adam and Eve knew that they had sinned, that they were guilty. And rather than face God and confess it, they attempted to hide from God.

This explains the attraction dimly lit nightspots hold for rebellious sinners. It also explains why some men lose themselves in their work. They are running from God.

David attempted to conceal his sin. The loyalty of Uriah to David not only frustrated his futile efforts at cover-up but also pointed up how sorry David's disloyalty to Uriah really was. In desperation David actually thought he could cover up his sin in the grave of Uriah. Nothing he tried could hide his sin from his own conscience or from God. Finally, after confession, David experienced the joy of forgiveness. This psalm is his testimony that there is no other way to deal with sin than to deal honestly with God. Honesty required acknowledgment of sin. Confession resulted in forgiveness. Forgiveness brought unbounding joy.

Until sin is dealt with honestly and forthrightly, it leaves a load of guilt upon the sinner. The cumulative weight of such guilt day after day can be overwhelming. Borne silently, carried alone, endured without relief, the burden of guilt distresses, depresses, and may even destroy a person. What can be done with guilt? It can be recognized for what it is: a dead weight upon those who sin and who refuse to confess it, be forgiven, and be cleansed. It can be dealt with in such a way as to get relief from it, no matter how grave the root cause. Ignoring sin will not cause it to go away. Left undealt with, it is like a spreading cancer sapping the very life out of a person.

The Blessedness of Forgiveness, 32:1–2

1. *Sin in Its Totalness* (vv. 1–2)

The psalm begins on a cheerful note, "Blessed." Clearly the sunshine of this blessed estate comes *after* the night of sin and guilt and struggle. This blessedness comes not from hiding sin or denying sin but by confessing sin.

Three words give the total picture of sin: "transgression,"

WHEN GUILT OVERWHELMS

which means rebellion; "sin," which means missing the mark; "iniquity," which means moral crookedness. "No deceit" means no insincerity or no self-deception. Absolute sincerity is the condition laid down for forgiveness to be complete. No matter what form nor how totally sinful a man might be, forgiveness is possible. When sought and experienced it is always a joyous event.

2. *Forgiveness in Its Completeness* (vv. 1-2)

Three words describe the completeness of the act of God in pardoning sin: "forgiven," which means lifted away by a vicarious sacrifice; "covered," which means hidden from the sight of God; and "cancelled," which means erased from God's record books. No one can miss his meaning. The forgiveness God effects is complete.

John wrote, "The blood of Jesus his Son cleanses us from all sin" (1 John 1:7). If your sins are not lifted away, covered over, and cancelled out by the Lamb of God, they will remain to crush you. Forgiveness, as the psalmist experienced it, did not mean that God obliterated the sin or blotted out the sinfiul deed and its effects so that what had been done was now undone. To the contrary, God took away the burden of guilt, delivered the psalmist from the agony of self-recrimination, and restored his relationship with God. The psalmist was still guilty. He was still a sinner. But he held in his hands the pardon papers. No wonder he was exultant!

3. *Happiness in Its Fullness* (vv. 1-2)

The word translated "blessed" is variously rendered by scholars and translators "happy," "oh, how happy," and so forth. The sinner so totally contaminated by sin found himself completely forgiven by the merciful God. No wonder he was so fully happy! The burden was lifted. The blight was covered. The books were cleared. The joy bells were ringing. Peace reigned in the psalmist's heart and mind.

The idea in "blessed" goes far beyond "happy." Other rooms in the house include "peace" and "freedom." When forgiveness is complete, peace, like the warm sun after a hard winter, permeates the total being of the person forgiven. Sin shackles a man as does a carpenter's vice. With every twist of the handle the grip tightens. It's like a rope with a slipknot around a calf's neck. Every tug of the calf tightens the rope and chokes off the air. But forgiveness untwists the handle, loosens the rope, and liberates the life. How good it is to breathe freely after days of struggle with the asthma of sin!

The Wretchedness of Impenitence, 32:3-4

1. *Wasting Away Under Impenitence* (v. 3)

At first David tried to cover his sin. When Uriah would not cooperate with his plot to cover up his sin with Bathsheba, David added murder to adultery and tried to bury his sin in Uriah's grave. But he discovered that his silence in failing to acknowledge his sin did not silence his conscience. The King James Version has "my bones waxed old." The Revised Standard Version has "my body wasted away." In the wake of David's silence, there came a withering away, an emptiness within, which penetrated to the core of his being. He groaned all day long, but not one word of confession escaped his lips. Failing strength and growing groans characterized David's sullen silence.

Why are we so hesitant to admit sin? It appears to be natural. Little children learn early to deny fault and to attempt to escape blame. My own children were not taught the art of buck-passing, but they mastered it at a tender age.

Can you picture this scene? All the children are in the kitchen. There's a buzz of talk and teasing as they are dishing

WHEN GUILT OVERWHELMS

up ice cream for an after-school snack. Suddenly there's a crash! Then silence! When their mother steps into the kitchen they chatter like a bunch of blackbirds, "I didn't do it! I didn't do it! She did it! He did it! It was his fault!" But the wise mother begins to talk to them about honesty and accepting responsibility. Soon the pain of guilt begins to show on the face of the real culprit. After suffering the pangs of conscience for a while, he confesses, "I did it. It was all my fault." And the tensions ease as they settle down to enjoy their ice cream.

2. *Weighed Down by God's Hand* (v. 4a)

Though David was silent, his conscience was not dead; and the hand of God was still upon him. Kyle Yates wrote, "That man is to be pitied who does not feel the hand of God upon him." [1] But for a season David remained in stubborn silence in spite of the increasing pressure of chastisement from God. How stubborn is man!

Some time back when news broke about one more political shenanigan, the congressman involved categorically denied personal relationship with his secretary. In only a few days he was in a hospital, overcome with guilt and attempting to silence his conscience and ease the pressure of God's hand upon him via sleeping pills. Later, he confessed an inappropriate involvement with his secretary.

Jot, of the Radio and Television Commission cartoon, reflects a finely honed conscience capable of inflicting intolerable pain. One scene has Jot exposed to the temptation of taking a cupcake just out of the oven. Unable to resist the lure of the cake, he took and ate it with delight. His mother noticed that the cupcake was missing. She asked Jot, "Did you take the cake?" He responded confidently, "No, ma'am!" A series of clips has Jot running at breakneck speed away from his mother, repeating louder and louder "No, ma'am!

No, ma'am!" Finally his conscience can stand it no longer. He stops, returns, and confesses, "I took it." With the psalmist we may conclude that the heavy hand of God was upon him.

3. *Dried Up as a Summer Heat* (v. 4*b*)

William Taylor interprets this entire psalm as an experience of extreme illness, confession of the sin that caused it, and complete healing following confession. Thus, the drying up of the psalmist's strength, he concludes, was caused by the fever of his disease.[2] The Hebrew text is obscure in this phrase. One manuscript has "my heart was changed to my ruin." Another has "my life sap was changed." The idea seems to be that his strength was spent as in summer's heat. It is a graphic picture of the debilitating effect of impenitence.

The effect of a high fever over several days is a drastic sapping of strength. Such a person may be weak and trembly for several days after the fever has subsided. If we are to interpret metaphorically, the psalmist was acknowledging a spiritual drought. The sin which caused his sickness had been like the searing sun, sapping his spiritual energy. Sin unconfessed has the same effect upon the soul (the inner life and vitality) of the sinner as a scorching summer sun has upon an unprotected plant. The plant wilts, droops, and looks lethargic.

The Effectiveness of Confession, 32:5–7

1. *Sin Acknowledged* (v. 5*a*)

David spent many miserable days and nights in stubborn silence. Finally, when he could stand the pressure no longer, he admitted his sins. According to the Samuel account, the prophet Nathan pointed the accusing finger at David in a public setting. "Thou art the man" was Nathan's charge.

WHEN GUILT OVERWHELMS

"I have sinned against the Lord" was David's confession (2 Sam. 12:13). Sin was the charge, and sin was what David acknowledged. He admitted that his deeds demonstrated that he was missing the mark. He had not yet learned how to live.

Here is revealed a significant mark of the character of David. He had sinned, but he was not above the law of cause and effect just because he was king of Judah. Neither was he beyond the principle of sin and judgment. He had to give an account to God just as any other man. One of the reasons David was called a man after God's own heart was his candid admission of sin.

2. *Iniquity Uncovered* (v. 5*b*)

What delayed confession and forgiveness was David's frantic effort to cover up his "iniquity," his moral crookedness. The moment he decided to quit trying to hide his sin from God, he was on the road to open confession and full forgiveness. As long as a man attempts to conceal his sin the road to confession and cleansing is blocked. John counseled, "If we confess our sins, he is faithful and just, and will forgive our sins and cleanse us from all unrighteousness" (1 John 1:9).

Moral crookedness is a blight on any man's character. It is especially reprehensible in a public official. When that public official is God's anointed king, it is intolerable. David lived in a fishbowl of exposure to his people. There was no way to hide his moral lapse for long.

3. *Transgression Confessed* (v. 5*c*)

Now the psalmist had called sin everything God calls it: "sin," "iniquity," "transgression." This represents a full confession, a clearing of the slate. Confession is not only open but also full, admitting to the whole range of sin against

God. Refusing to admit sin, standing to defend our sins, trying to rationalize our sins, we remain under the burden of guilt and the pressure of chastisement. The only road to release, to life, and to happiness is confession.

We have a saying, "Confession is good for the soul." And it is. The tight fist of rebellion is relaxed upon confession. The bad aim of life which results in repeatedly missing the mark can be adjusted. The erratic life-style of moral crookedness is smoothed out. Since sin is essentially against God, confession is to be to God. This is not to suggest that the principle of confessing our faults one to another is not therapeutic. It is. But the first offense is against God.

4. *Forgiveness Effected* (v. 5*d*)

The language shows the close tie between confession and forgiveness. Leupold says, "The forgiveness followed hard on the heels of the confession." [3] He offers this paraphrase to show the connection: "As soon as I said, I will confess, Thou forgavest." Simple, sincere confession met with prompt, direct response. Paul used this psalm (vv. 1–2) to argue forcefully for the doctrine of salvation by free grace alone (Rom. 4:7–8).

The author of Proverbs pointed out the relationship between confession and forgiveness: "He who conceals his transgressions will not prosper, but he who confesses and forsakes them will obtain mercy" (Prov. 28:13). The psalmist said the Lord forgave "the guilt of my sin." Confession, forgiveness, removal of guilt—they all go together. To say that the psalmist confessed is to suggest that he had repented. Now he was free from the burden of sin. The peace in his heart testified to the forgiveness of his guilt.

5. *Principle Stated* (v. 6)

Based on his experience, the poet exhorted others to learn

from his error. He realized the misery of silence in the face of sin. The principle he urged was, "At the time of finding, confess." Don't delay! Don't conceal it! Be prompt to confess sin.

The person who stays up to date with God through confession will know uninterrupted preservation from outward disasters. At the same time he will remain inwardly unassailable by affliction and danger. This is not to say that they will not come. But the believer is safe in Christ. He is kept by the power of God.

6. *Deliverance Shouted* (v. 7)

God is the hiding place for sinners. We are hid with Christ in God. He is the key to the preservation of the saints. We are preserved by the power of God from trouble. We are surrounded by the shouts of deliverance. O the utter happiness of a man whose sins are forgiven! That's shouting ground!

Therefore, shouts of deliverance in praise of God form the only appropriate response from a forgiven heart. Our hymn expresses it well:

> Rock of Ages, cleft for me,
> Let me hide myself in Thee;
> Let the water and the blood,
> From Thy wounded side which flowed,
> Be of sin the double cure,
> Save from wrath and make me pure.
>
> Nothing in my hand I bring,
> Simply to Thy cross I cling;
> Naked, come to Thee for dress,
> Helpless, look to Thee for grace;
> Foul, I to the fountain fly,
> Wash me, Saviour, or I die.

And when he does, that's worth shouting about.

The Insightfulness of God's Counsel, 32:8-9

1. *Full Knowledge of the Way of God* (v. 8)

Some interpreters take these two verses to be a description of the psalmist's willingness to share his experience. It seems better to accept these as the poet's report of the insight which God gave him. God promised to instruct and teach David the way he should walk. Forgiven men are not free from allurement to walk the wrong way. A tragic failure of churches is to assume that young Christians will naturally follow the ways of Christ if only they can be converted to Christ. Conversion comes in a moment. Learning to walk with Christ is a lifetime project.

How does one go about gaining full knowledge of the ways of God? What avenues are open to God in his teaching role in our lives? We do not expect an audible voice or a visual appearance of God. Actually the door to God's instruction is opened as widely or closed as tightly as we desire. We have the Bible; but it must be read, studied, reflected upon, applied. We must get a grip on it and allow it to get a grip on us. There are people, teachers, pastors, books, and experiences available to us; but we must take advantage of these. One cannot walk in God's ways if he does not know them. He cannot know them without some openness and effort on his part to learn.

2. *Careful Guidance with the Eye of God* (v. 8b)

How does God guide with his eye? We sing about God's hand leading us. But how? Perhaps the best insight into God's guiding with the eye is the snapshot of Peter which Luke preserved for us after Peter had denied Jesus (Luke 22:61). The text says, "And the Lord turned and looked at Peter." Without a word having passed, Peter remembered the Lord's previous warning and was so convicted and chas-

WHEN GUILT OVERWHELMS

tened that he went out and wept bitterly.

To receive guidance from God's eye suggests the necessity of being close enough to see his eye, submissive enough to look to him for guidance, and intimate enough to understand such communication. Have you not observed with interest the way a husband and wife often communicate with one another in social settings without use of words? So intimate are they, so well are their likes and dislikes shown to each other, that a look, a facial expression, or a gesture communicates clearly. Only the truly intimate can communicate in this manner.

3. *Abrupt Warning About Following God* (v. 9)

The alternative to the gentle guidance God delights to give his children (with his eye) is the harsh treatment required to guide a brute beast. Bits and bridles are used to force horses to do as a man demands. Kyle Yates suggests, "Men who refuse to come to God in penitence and obey His wishes naturally lower themselves to the level of brute beasts and must expect severe discipline." [4] Thus God warns those who have been forgiven not to forget God's mercy to them and not to be like brute beasts.

Even a brute beast can be trained to follow his master without the discipline of a bridle. One of the chief delights of my children while they were very small was to go to "Paw-pe's house" in the country and ride the Shetland pony he kept for the grandchildren through the years. After hours of their coaxing the pony by tugging on the reins, he finally learned to walk obediently behind whoever was leading him around the yard. If the visit lasted for several days, the pony would follow the leader even when the reins were in the rider's hands. God warned the psalmist not to be like a stubborn mule but to stay close to God, the source of righteousness, comfort, and mercy.

The Joyfulness of the Righteous, 32:10–11

1. *Sharp Pangs for the Wicked* (v. 10*a*)

Misery is the lot of those who refuse to be led into the experience of forgiveness. By contrast, mercy is the lot of those who continue to trust in the Lord.

2. *Steady Love for the Trusting* (v. 10*b*)

The sufferings of the wicked are "many." The surroundings of the trusting are *chesed*. This word is untranslatable. It has been rendered "mercy" (KJV), "steadfast love" (RSV) "unfailing love" (NEB), and "lovingkindness" (ASV). It is regularly used to describe God's fidelity to the covenant relationship with Israel.

The person who continues to put his trust in the Lord will be surrounded by love. This is a special kind of love, reserved for those in covenant relationship with God. The word rendered "trust" is a participle, suggesting continuous action. Only the person who goes on trusting the Lord constantly experiences a relationship completely saturated by love. This is no soap-opera, sentimental type of love, selfish and emotional. Rather, it is clear-eyed, unselfish, and other-oriented. This is the kind of love that always looks out for the best interests of the one loved.

3. *Shouts of Joy for the Upright* (v. 11)

The righteous ones, those put right with God through forgiveness, are exhorted to be glad and to rejoice in the Lord. Durham suggests, "The most illuminating aspect of these verses (vv. 10–11) is the poet's triple affirmation that joy in Yahweh belongs only to him who has first been honest with Yahweh."[5] Rejoicing is reserved for the righteous!

Thus, the psalmist closed on the note with which he began. "Blessed" is the first word. "Shout for joy" is the last. In between is reported the author's overwhelming bout with sin and guilt. He set out to hide his sin from God with damaging results. When he confessed his sin, he discovered that God was a hiding place for him. From that vantage point he exhorted the righteous (of whom he was one) to "be glad in the Lord," to "rejoice," and to "shout for joy." When guilt overwhelms a person, the best thing to do is to deal with it. Confess, experience forgiveness, and shout for joy!

8
When Needs Are Numerous

Psalm 23

Without a doubt this is the pearl of the Psalms, the most popular of all. Many people memorize its marvelous lines in childhood. And when they do, its promise of the presence of God to provide all their needs ministers assurance, comfort, and hope throughout life. Across twenty-two years of pastoral ministry, this psalm was requested more often than any other portion of Scripture, as I attempted to comfort the sorrowing, counsel the troubled, minister to those lacking physical necessities, and encourage the sick.

The majority of interpreters find only one figure—the shepherd—in the psalm. Some see two—the shepherd and the host. Others insert a third between these two—the guide. It seems best to interpret the psalm as a unity under one figure, the shepherd. J. Wash Watts not only saw a single figure in the psalm but he also interpreted that one to be the Messiah. Thus, according to him the theme is "The Good Shepherd," obviously influenced by Jesus' assertion about himself: "I am the good shepherd" (John 10:11). To say that the ideas in the psalm are perfectly fulfilled in Christ is one thing. But to say that the psalmist wrote consciously to describe the Messiah's ministry is another. It is correct to see fulfillment in Christ. But the psalmist probably did not have this in mind. We who have the New Testament can clearly see God's working in behalf of his creatures.

Provider, 23:1

1. *Covenant God* (v. 1*a*)

A little girl, asked to quote her favorite Scripture, responded, "The Lord is my shepherd; he's all I want." And he is all she needs.

The Lord, Yahweh, Israel's covenant God, was the psalmist's shepherd. What an assertion! Ezekiel predicted a day when God would shepherd the nation (Ezek. 34:11–16). But the psalmist, as an individual, claimed Yahweh as his shepherd. Leupold says the name Yahweh "always connotes God's absolute faithfulness to His people." [1]

The first interest of a good shepherd was to supply the sheep with everything necessary to their well-being. Since Yahweh was the psalmist's shepherd, he could confidently assert, "I shall not want." Everyone who can truthfully say, "The Lord is my shepherd," can boldly declare, "I shall not want." Paul understood this relationship. He gave expression to his faith in these words: "But my God shall supply all your need according to his riches in glory by Christ Jesus" (Phil. 4:19, KJV).

To properly call the Lord "my" shepherd requires personal faith. Only children born or adopted into my family may fittingly call me Father. Only persons willing to renounce allegiance to all other princes, kings, and potentates and who pledge allegiance to the United States of America can claim citizenship in our great country.

Similarly, only those who are born into God's family may properly call him Father. He is shepherd only to the sheep who are committed followers. Jesus said, "My sheep hear my voice, and I know them, and they follow me" (John 10:27). Sheep recognize the voice of their shepherd. They respond only to their shepherd. The shepherd knows his own sheep intimately by name, markings, and habits. Only the sheep that actually follow the shepherd enjoy the benefits of the shepherd's care.

2. *Complete Care* (v. 1*c*)

The psalmist's assertion "I shall not want" was a confession of his faith. It meant that he was trusting the shepherd for all his needs. In Israel's wilderness experience, the Lord provided manna from heaven. Providing one day's portion for one day's need was apparently designed to teach the people to trust him daily. Jesus taught his disciples to pray, "Give us this day our daily bread" (Matt. 6:11). The psalmist's experience of no deficiency in any area of need led him to expect a future characterized by complete care.

Jesus wants his disciples to learn to live one day at a time, leaning on him. He feeds the birds and dresses the lilies. How much more will he care for the needs of his people! How foolish to worry about food, clothing, and shelter for the day! And more foolish still to worry about tomorrow! He is eminently able as a provider.

Provisions, 23:2–3*a*

1. *Rest* (v. 2*a*)

For a sheep to "lie down" indicated that it was tired. But for it to lie down in green pastures suggested that it was full, also. It was satisfied. The language suggests a frequentative idea. The shepherd made the sheep lie down to rest again and again. The picture is this: The shepherd had led the sheep to forage for grass in a scanty pastureland. Hours passed. The sun was hot. The sheep were exhausted. The shepherd was resourceful. He found a grassy meadow. After the sheep have eaten to the full, he provided the needed rest.

How wise the shepherd was to schedule the rest before the "straight paths" of the afternoon and the "deep darkness" of the evening! He knew the road ahead. He saw the end from the beginning and all the events in between. Tomorrow, with its demands of strength and stamina, was in his eyes as clearly as today. If he provided a rest, there was probably a good reason. Wise sheep would do well to rest.

2. *Refreshment* (v. 2*b*)

This line adds another feature to the rest stop, water. By regular use, certain resting places became traditional. These places were habitually used because they were safe and the water supply was sufficient. "Still waters" (KJV, RSV) is literally "waters of rest." "Resting place with water" is the idea. In such a setting the sheep were refreshed and made ready for the remainder of the day.

Those who live in extremely low rainfall areas can appreciate this experience of the sheep better than those of us who live along the coast. However, anyone who has gone very long without water should have some ability to identify with the refreshment that comes from satisfying one's thirst with cool water. After rapid water loss through perspiration, an athlete is refreshed by drinking water. A farmer or hunter can appreciate the thirst for water, since both may go for several hours without water. Nothing tastes as good or satisfies as completely as cool water when one is thirsty.

3. *Restoration* (v. 3*a*)

Instead of changing figures as some interpreters insist, the psalmist introduced what Leupold calls a "nonfigurative statement of spiritual values." [2] This reminds us that the shepherd was concerned with more than meeting material needs. And even more importantly, it alerts us to the fact that we aren't reading about a shepherd and his sheep but about the Lord and his people.

Nephesh may be properly translated "life" and relates to

physical revival and restoration. Again the language suggests a frequentative idea. Over and over life is restored. But it seems more is here than that. I believe spiritual restoration is in focus in this line.

Paths, 23:3*b*

1. *Competent Guide* (v. 3*b*)

"He leads me" points to the shepherd as the guide. Sheep with no sense of direction were lost without a guide. "Paths of righteousness" may be rendered "right paths," but emphasis seems to be on the righteousness of the guide, and only secondarily on the kind of path chosen. Rest was not an end in itself. It was an "in order to" kind of thing. The refreshment and restoration of the rest were to get one ready for the road ahead.

Good counsel to modern sheep is to take advantage of every opportunity to enrich life, to gain knowledge of the word of God, to mature as a follower of Jesus Christ. The Lord is probably getting you ready for the road ahead, perhaps a rough road.

2. *Chosen Paths* (v. 3*b*)

As the shepherd chose the path for the sheep, so the Lord selects the route for pilgrims. Sheep, with no direction-finding equipment and no defensive ability, must rely completely on the competence of the shepherd. Actually, there is a double choice. The Lord in his wisdom chooses what is best for us. Then we must choose to follow his leadership. We are not forced. He leads! He does not push!

"Paths of righteousness" may mean "straight paths" in the sense of a hard road to follow. Life is not a bed of roses for most of us. Usually there are thorns among the roses. Illness may come and with it our world may come crashing down at our feet. Death of one dear to us may be along

WHEN NEEDS ARE NUMEROUS

tomorrow's path and bring in its wake overpowering sorrow. But along such a path one does not have to go alone. If the shepherd puts such shattering things along the path, he is not thereby proved incompetent. Instead, he is revealing his competence. He is giving an opportunity for growth, if met successfully, in an area of life where tomorrow's demands will require such growth.

3. *Consistent Purpose* (v. 3c)

"For his name's sake" means for God's sake or for God's established purpose and reputation of loyalty to his people. Every path he chooses for us is consistent with his purpose for us. What he chooses may not always seem good. It may not be our first choice. But it will always work out for the best. It is Paul's affirmation: "We know that in everything God works for good with those who love him, who are called according to his purpose" (Rom. 8:28).

We say we are having a good day when everything is going "our" way. If everything is "coming up roses," we declare that God is good and that he is evidently working out his good plan for our lives. But when shadows fall across our path, we conclude that we have fallen out of God's favor. Right? Could I suggest consideration of a wild idea? Is it not possible that God is working as faithfully and as much in accord with his purpose for us on our cloudy days as on our sunshiny days? I believe so.

Some things are learned through adversity and can be learned in no other way. If what God does through our experience of adversity is ultimately good for us, is not even the day of adversity a good day? Shock and grief had numbed the household when I arrived at the home of what was now a very young widow. Her husband had topped the hill of a narrow blacktop road near Homer, Louisiana, where he met another vehicle head-on on his side of the road. He was killed instantly. As I sat beside the young widow, I did not say: "Congratulations; your husband is dead. Now you are left to raise your little children alone; that's good." No, no, no, a thousand times, no! But I did say, "Let God be in this by your faith-openness to him. He has promised to work even under these circumstances for your good."

Perils, 23:4

1. *Prevalence of Shadows* (v. 4a)

To be a sheep in Palestine was to live a perilous life. There were ravenous beasts ready to pounce on the helpless sheep in an unguarded moment. There were deep ravines into which sheep might fall. To be a follower of Jesus Christ in our time is fraught with perils, too. Contrary to the concept of some, being a believer does not inoculate one against the trials, troubles, and perils common to other men. "Into each life some light must shine" is a true statement. But it is equally true to say, "Into each life some darkness, sometimes deep darkness, must fall." Suffering and sorrow come upon us all.

Instead of "though," we would be true to experience to translate "when." Sooner or later—if not both sooner and later—we are certain to have our days of sorrow, suffering, and darkness. "Shadow of death" is "deep darkness," including death at the end of the way. But it also covers the difficulties, distresses, and darknesses all along the way. "Walk" is a frequentative imperfect. This suggests experience after experience of walking through deep darkness. Again and again the nearness of the Shepherd banishes fear.

2. *Presence of the Shepherd* (v. 4b)

The primary reason the psalmist could say "I will fear no evil" was that he was so confident when he said, "Thou art with me." There is little comfort in the clichés friends

WHEN NEEDS ARE NUMEROUS

sincerely recite as you face great perils. Someone will say, when dark clouds descend, "Every cloud has a silver lining." This doesn't help much. What helps most of all is to be conscious of the nearness of the Shepherd. A note of encouragement is found in the word "through." It implies emergence on the other side. But the greatest encouragement is the assurance that one does not have to walk the dark valley alone. A familiar song reminds us of just how individual death is:

> You got to walk that lonesome valley,
> You got to go there by yo'self;
> No one here can go there for you,
> You got to go there by yo' self.[3]

But the Christian does not walk it alone! The poet wrote:

> My plans were made, I thought my path
>   all bright and clear,
> My heart with song o'er flowed, the
>   world seemed full of cheer.
> My Lord I wished to serve, to take Him
>   for my guide;
> To keep so close that I could feel Him
>   by my side.
>   And so I traveled on.
>
> But suddenly, in skies so clear and full
>   of light,
> The clouds fell thick and fast, the days
>   seemed changed to night;
> Instead of paths so clear and full of
>   things so sweet,
> Rough things and thorns and stones
>   seemed all about my feet;
>   I scarce could travel on.
>
> I bowed my head and wondered why this
>   change should come.
> And murmured—"Lord, is this because
>   of aught I've done?

> Has not the path been full enough
>   of pain and care?
> Why should not my path again be
>   changed from dark to fair?"
>   But still I traveled on.
>
> I listened—quiet and still, there came
>   a voice—
> "This path is mine, not thine, I
>   made the choice;
> Dear child, this service will be best
>   for thee and me,
> If thou wilt simply trust, and leave
>   the end to me."
>   And so we traveled on.[4]

3. *Protection of the Sheep* (v. 4c)

In addition to the presence of the shepherd to relieve fear, there was also the protection, strengthening, and comfort of the sheep through the shepherd's use of the rod and the staff. With his rod the shepherd beat off the enemies of the sheep, and with his staff he helped them through the dark and perilous paths. Jesus, the good shepherd, said, "No one shall snatch them out of my hand" (John 10:28). The sheep are safe in the shepherd's care.

Whether a shepherd typically carried two instruments or only one is not critical to a proper interpretation of the thoughts expressed by "rod" and "staff." Some shepherds were equipped with a long stick with a crook on one end called a staff. In addition to the staff on which the shepherd leaned for his own support and with which he guided or rescued the sheep, another instrument was frequently carried. It was small compared to the shepherd's crook and was heavy on one end. Sometimes it was reinforced with nails driven into the heavy end. This rod was a kind of club used to defend the sheep when a wild animal attacked the flock.

In the midst of dangers the sheep were comforted by the shepherd's rod and staff. With the rod the sheep were kept safe from marauding enemies, and with the staff they were kept close in to the shepherd. The sheep benefited alike from great deliverances from deadly enemies and from gentle discipline when drifting from the shepherd's care.

Preparation, 23:5

1. *Providing the Table* (v. 5 *a*)

Instead of a change of figure to an Oriental host, the shepherd motif may still prevail. It was not uncommon for the shepherd to take along supplementary food for days when the grass was limited. In such an event the shepherd provided a table, a large strip of leather laid on the ground. Though only the table is mentioned, food is certainly implied.

By not mentioning food specifically, the psalmist might have meant to magnify that other dominant feature of festive occasions, fellowship. If banqueting is the metaphor, when the food is taken away, all that is left is fellowship. To switch metaphors here leaves an odd caricature of a shepherd, however. It would be strange to have a shepherd who was only concerned with leading the sheep and who showed no interest in feeding the sheep. The shepherd usually led the sheep into green pastures where food was more than adequate. But suppose there were no green pastures? The shepherd was resourceful. He carried reserve fodder for such days.

2. *Preparing the Guest* (v. 5 *b*)

The verb describing the anointing of the head is a perfect in the Hebrew, perhaps handled correctly by Leupold as follows, "Thou hast already anointed my head with oil." [5] This was a courtesy afforded by the host to all honored guests at a banquet. It reflected the attitude of the host toward the guest and signaled admittance to the banquet table. But it may be descriptive of the shepherd's practice of carrying a little flask of oil to doctor the face of the sheep, often scratched by foraging for food among the thorns and brambles.

Whichever figure you choose, the role of the shepherd or host is the same—that of preparing the sheep/guest for participation at the table. "My enemies" may refer to enemies of the sheep lurking in the shadows as the shepherd spreads the table and the sheep eat under his protective care. The phrase may picture the guest secure in the home of the host while the enemies of the guest look on, helpless to do harm to the guest. The enemies have not been invited. They are shut out of that fellowship.

3. *Pouring the Cup* (v. 5c)

The psalmist seemed overwhelmed with the adequacy—yea, the extravagance—of the shepherd. It was more than he could take in. His cup was full to overflowing. A gospel song expressed it well:

> Fill my cup, Lord;
> I lift it up, Lord.
> Come and quench this thirsting
>   of my soul.
> Bread of heaven, feed me
>   till I want no more;
> Fill my cup,
>   Fill it up, and make me whole.[6]

Prospect, 23:6

1. *Daily Attendants* (v. 6a)

"Surely" suggests certainty, and this could be the idea. But the word may also mean "only." This would confess the faith of the psalmist. God would see to it that out of

WHEN NEEDS ARE NUMEROUS

all the things that might happen to him, only goodness and steadfast love would be his daily attendants. Is it best to take these daily attendants in an abstract sense, goodness and mercy in general? Or is it best to take the words in a more particular reference to the goodness and mercy of God?

The latter seems best. Amos equated the goodness of God with God himself (Amos 5:4,6,14). Goodness as an attendant may mean that God is the daily attendant. What a prospect! "Mercy" is the translation of the Hebrew word regularly used to refer to God's love in his covenant bond with Israel. It is descriptive of God's loyal love for his covenant people. Indeed, what a glorious prospect! And what a testimony to the faith of the psalmist!

2. *Durable Attachment* (v. 6 *b*)

"Dwell in the house of the Lord" is taken by some interpreters as a clue that David did not write this psalm. The Temple had not been built, they say. However, this expression need not be exhausted by the idea of physical presence in the literal Temple. Communion with God may be the idea. In flight from his angered brother, Esau, Jacob lay down at the end of a long day to rest. His sleep was disturbed by a startling dream. He had successfully escaped from the hand of his brother, but he had not left God behind. He was out of the reach of his brother, but he was not out of touch with God.

God had a plan which included Jacob. It concerned a promise made to his grandfather, Abraham, and passed on to his father, Isaac. There was a promised land, a people, and a purpose to bless all the families of the earth. And on top of all that, God's presence with Jacob was promised as the guarantee of fulfillment. No wonder Jacob raised his head from his stone pillar to exclaim, "Surely the Lord is in this place; and I did not know it" (Gen. 28:16). Then as his head cleared completely he declared, "How awesome is this place! This is none other than the house of God, and this is the gate of heaven" (Gen. 28:17). Anywhere a man meets God is "the house of God."

Surely a lasting fellowship and permanent residence with God are implied by the words "for ever." This psalmist was convinced that the presence of God which he enjoyed daily would not end with "all the days of his life." Thus, he held out the prospect of an eternal fellowship with Yahweh, his shepherd. "For ever" is literally "for length of days." But the idea is not simply "as long as I live" here on earth. Already he had expressed his faith and assurance about daily fellowship with God (v. 6 a). The reference in this part of the verse expands the idea of uninterrupted fellowship daily to uninterrupted fellowship throughout eternity. Never, never would he be alone, now as a pilgrim or hereafter as a permanent resident in God's household.

9
When Praise Is Missing

Psalm 103

The sheer beauty of this psalm has made it an all-time favorite. Leupold calls it "a pure note of praise." [1] Taylor claims that it is "one of the noblest hymns in the Old Testament." [2] Oesterley wrote, "In words as beautiful as any in the Psalter, the psalmist tells of the love of God toward those who fear him." [3] Yates concludes, "No purer outburst of praise and gratitude can be found in all the Scriptures." [4]

Griffith was discerning when he observed: "A single theme runs through this mighty anthem of praise—the theme of God's grace." He goes on to define grace as "something extra in life, . . . the way (God) deals with us beyond our deserving, the good things he gives us, not because he has to give them but because he wants to give them." [5] He derives a single admonition from the psalmist's treatment of this theme: Don't underestimate God!

Christians may be more accustomed to making petitions to God than praising God. Jesus encouraged this when he said, "Ask . . . seek . . . knock." And James rebukes us with his "Ye have not because ye ask not." Even so, most Christians I know seem more comfortable with petitions than praise. Perhaps the psalmist was admitting that the flower of gratitude to God was not growing in his garden. Thus, he called upon his own soul to express praise to God for his grace. But he didn't stop there. He realized that many of the good things in his life have come to him because of his attachment to God's chosen nation. Thus, he recited the blessings of God upon Israel. But he didn't stop there. He had gained insight into the sweep of God's kingdom, which caused him to call upon heaven and earth to praise God.

Personal Praise, 103:1-5

1. *All One's Being* (v. 1)

"Soul" and "all that is within me" combine to mean whole personality and entire inner being. The kind of praise called for is not superficial—"from the teeth out," as we say. Some of the "P.T.L. anyhow" enthusiasts turn me off, making praise a mockery instead of a meaningful, heart-felt expression. J. Wash Watts says, "To bless means to pronounce holy." [6] The root means "to bend the knee, to kneel." In the piel stem, it means to praise, to adore, to bless God. It is a piel imperative here. So the psalmist was commanding his own soul to express praise, to pronounce blessing.

The blessing was for Yahweh, the covenant God of Israel. It is for "his holy name." "Name" means his character as "holy," according to his revelation of himself in his dealings with man. To him whose name is above every name, holy, set apart, other, distinctive, the psalmist would ascribe sincere praise. The basis for blessing God in this verse is God himself. Because of who he is he is due our blessing and praise. He is the Lord; he is holy; he is worthy.

2. *All God's Benefits* (vv. 2-5)

Parents prompt their children to be grateful, to express appreciation, to say thank you, lest the children develop the attitude of ingrates. For the third time the psalmist issued a self-exhortation. "Bless the Lord, O my soul." Then he added the basis for blessing, "And forget not all his benefits." Derek Kinder explains, *"Benefits* is the noun that corre-

WHEN PRAISE IS MISSING

sponds to the fervent phrase in 13:6, 'he has dealt bountifully with me.' " [7] Hezekiah, king of Judah, forgot to praise God because "his heart was proud" (2 Chron. 32:25). It was not that he absentmindedly forgot God's miraculous restoration to health after his sickness to the point of death. Pride crept in, and he forgot. We all tend to take for granted the blessings that come to us often. How long has it been since you praised God for life, health, clean air, job, family, friends, food? What are some of those other benefits?

A. *Forgiveness* (v. 3a). The foremost blessing for poor sinners is the forgiveness of iniquity. This benefit stands first in the list because it is first in importance. Generally, if a person cannot praise God for forgiving his sins, he will not praise him for anything else. The establishment of a right relationship to God is prerequisite to the expression of praise. The ground for praising God for forgiveness is twofold: (1) It is entirely undeserved; and (2) "all iniquity," not just some, or the worst, but *all* is forgiven. So often adults bring a childlike "me do it" attitude to the business of dealing with sin. But there is no basis for personal merit in securing forgiveness. None of us deserve it.

B. *Healing* (v. 3b). Only the person who has suffered severe illness and who has experienced recovery from it can truly appreciate the benefit of healing. Based on experience and medical acknowledgment in some circles, I am convinced that a good case of Christianity would prepare the way for clearing out about half the patients now occupying hospital beds. This is not to suggest that they are not really sick. They are. But the cure is spiritual in nature, not physiological. For some time now physicians have recognized the tie between physical and mental health. A fairly new thrust in medicine today is to recognize that a man's spiritual condition may have a bearing on his mental and physical health. Have you praised God for your good health lately?

C. *Redemption* (v. 4 a). "Pit" could refer to the grave or death. It is from a verb meaning "corruption" or "destruction." To "redeem" is to buy back and suggests rescue of life from the possessive hands of death. Derek Kinder thinks that it is not only possible but also probable that the larger question of ransom from death and continuance of life forever—that is, resurrection to eternal life—is the particular benefit described here (Ps. 16:9–11).[8] Whether or not that is so, it is certain that redemption of life from destructive and corruptive forces is a praiseworthy benefit Christians enjoy. How blessed is the child whose home is cast like a protective canopy over him in his tender years! How blessed is a community where the powerful and pervasive influence of Christians crowds out corruptive forces of evil! Removal of the influence of Christians from society would plunge the world into a nightmare of moral chaos.

D. *Crown* (v. 4 b). The crown is not of gold befitting a king but a crown of "steadfast love and mercy" suited to the needs of the children of God. The psalmist praised God that he surrounded him with these spiritual benefits. This is like icing on the cake. Do you see the poet's picture? His paint splashed lavishly in first one direction and then another, portraying a God who forgives, heals, redeems, and, now on top of it all, "crowns with steadfast love and mercy."

E. *Satisfaction* (v. 5a). As a man's hunger is satisfied with good food, so the psalmist's needs were satisfied by God's benefits. The Hebrew text is obscure in this verse. The King James Version has "mouth," while the Revised Standard Version translators emended the text to read "as long as you live." What is clear in the verse is that God's goodness satisfies his children. Made for God, man is restless, unfulfilled, until he finds rest in God. Our rootless and restless generation may be explained on this basis. Searching for the good in

WHEN PRAISE IS MISSING

life in the wrong place is bound to result in restlessness. Finding the good should end the aimless drifting and anchor that one to the Rock of Ages.

F. *Renewal* (v. 5 *b*). In addition to satisfying, the goodness of God renews the life "like the eagle's." The eagle was used as a regular metaphor for renewed vigor. Yates comments, "The psalmist is thanking God that he has eternal springtime in his heart." [9]

The telltale signs of age creeping up on us strike anxious fear in our hearts. Scientists generally and the medical profession particularly are concerned with aging. Research continues to probe the causes of aging and to seek to retard or reverse the aging process. Ponce de Leon was not the first or the last explorer to go in search of a fountain of youth. For our poet, the renewal of youthful vigor was to be found in God.

National Praise, 103:6–18

Some benefits we receive from God are of a personal nature. They come out of direct relationship to him. Other benefits from God accrue to us because we belong to a particular nation. Our poet's thoughts now turned in the latter direction. The shift is from personal benefits to national blessings. The psalmist had been the recipient of these benefits, too. Having just celebrated two hundred years of freedom as a nation, I am more keenly aware than ever before of the benefits that are mine because I am an American. Freedom of speech, freedom of the press, free enterprise, freedom of worship—all of these and many more blessings are ours because we are citizens of the United States of America. I can praise God for that.

1. *Deliverance for the Oppressed* (v. 6)

Reference to the "oppressed" is not a generalization. It

is not merely a truism. The nation of Israel had been in bondage in Egypt. They had suffered injustices and oppression. They cried out to God. He heard their prayers and sent Moses to rescue them. By a series of plagues God pressured Pharaoh to release his captive people. Yahweh worked righteousness and justice for the oppressed. He delivered them from bondage.

The Bible regularly represents God as taking the side of the downtrodden, the have-nots, and the uncelebrated. God disapproves of those who take advantage of the disadvantaged. In the eighth century B.C., Amos cried out against those who would "sell the righteous for silver,/ and the needy for a pair of shoes—/ they that trample the head of the poor into the dust of the earth" (Amos 2:6–7). Oppressed people have a special place in the heart of God.

The author of Exodus stacked up words to display the response of God to his suffering people. He said, "God heard their groaning . . . remembered his covenant . . . . saw the people . . . knew their condition" (Ex. 2:24). When God called Moses to be the human agent of Israel's deliverance, God reminded Moses, "I know their sufferings, and I have come down to deliver them" (Ex. 3:7–8). God knows when we suffer. He cares and comes to deliver.

2. *Direction for His People* (v. 7)

Direction was given through a director, Moses, to whom the Lord made known "his ways." Some interpreters understand "his ways" to mean "his methods of dealing with men" and not the ways he would have them go (see 33:13). However, it seems best to understand "his directions for life." Moses asked God to show him his ways in order that God might be known to Moses and that he and Israel as a nation might find favor in God's sight. Isaiah predicted a day when Yahweh worship would be exalted, when the nations would be attracted to it, when they would learn the Torah (God's teachings) and walk in his paths. Revelation is never for entertainment or for God's people to be so bedazzled that they respond with, "Wow!" The ways of God are for following.

God's "acts" in behalf of "the sons of Israel" demonstrated his authority to give direction to their lives. "Acts" is best understood as the marvels and wonders of the ten plagues, the opening of the sea, the provision of food and water, the victory over Amalek, the revelation of the Ten Words, and so on. Both Moses and Miriam (his sister) led Israel in singing praises to God their great deliverer. In all of the "acts" of God in behalf of Israel, he was directing them to a mountain, to a covenant, to a land, to a missionary purpose. God had been good to the nation. For these blessings he was praised.

3. *Depository of His Love* (vv. 8–11)

Verse 8 and following appears to be a quotation from Exodus 34:6–7. "Merciful and gracious" are God's words, describing the kind of God he is. The psalmist was reciting a revelation Israel had already received. God abounds in "steadfast love." This is not a shotgun blast of love aimed at no one in particular. It is a rifle shot of love, especially exercised "toward those who fear him" (v. 11). The backdrop of Exodus 34 is the calf incident, representing the rebellion of the people against God and his leader, Moses. As a result of that rebellion the covenant was broken, dramatically symbolized by Moses' act of crashing the tables of stone (containing the Ten Commandments) upon the ground. But God is merciful and gracious, slow to anger, and abounding in steadfast love. God cannot abandon them. His love will not allow it.

This mercy, grace, and love was manifest in a kind of

restraint upon God. He is said to be "slow to anger"; "he will not always chide" (though he has reason to strive with Israel, he will not do so); "he will not keep his anger for ever"; "he does not deal with us according to our sins, nor requite us according to our iniquities." Israel had experienced God's love in many ways and found it to be great like the heavens "high above the earth." "Slow to anger" is literally "long of nostrils," which suggests the positive quality of patience. "Chide" translates a word used for disputes, especially at law. To "not keep his anger for ever" means that God does not nurse his grievances against us. Man is prone to keep things stirred up, not God. If he dealt with us with the severity our sins would merit, none of us could survive. Thankfully, his ways are higher than our ways. He delights to show love to those who reverence him.

4. *Distance Between Us and Our Sins* (v. 12)

Sin separates us from God. After their sin, Adam and Eve hid in an effort to put distance between them and God. Ultimately they were cast out of the Garden, out of touch with the tree of life, and out of fellowship with God. Our poet reveals that God's great love for us causes him to separate our sins from us an immeasurable distance, "as far as the east is from the west." So separated, sin cannot harm us.

How far is it from east to west? A mathematician would answer, "Infinity separates the east from the west." The space is unlimited. Though the poet was not attempting to speak with scientific accuracy, he was stating categorically that God's removal of sin is complete, thorough, adequate. So far removed is sin that it cannot possibly have any further impact on the life of the sinner. Upon man's confession and repentance, God dispenses with sin completely.

WHEN PRAISE IS MISSING 121

wait upon him. In what sense precisely they "carry out his will" is not described. But whatever was meant, the psalmist's main point is clear. Since God's rule extends over all, every aspect of creation is due to offer him praise.

"All his works" is a catchall phrase, just in case anyone or anything has been overlooked. The whole universe over which God reigns is called upon to praise God. The psalm ends as it began, with a self-exhortation: "Bless the Lord, O my soul." It is as if to say, *If no one else does, I will praise the Lord.* And yet the psalmist knew that he was not singing a solo. All the things and beings God has created unite in a vast harmony of praise to the Creator.

Just as the psalmists learned that they were not alone in meeting the stresses and strains of the daily grind of life, we too can know that no experience of ours need ever be outside his concern and care. Remember, when God seems far away, if prayers seem blocked, doubts arise, troubles come, sickness strikes, fears dismay, guilt overwhelms, or needs are numerous, that God is near. He knows. He cares. He comes to us where we are, at our point of need. His resources are inexhaustible. His care is complete. Appropriate response on our part is praise.

Psalm 150 exhorts us to praise God everywhere, under all circumstances, with all available instruments:

> Praise the Lord!
> Praise God in his sanctuary;
>   praise him in his mighty firmament!
> Praise him for his mighty deeds;
>   praise him according to his
>   exceeding greatness!
> Praise him with trumpet sound;
>   praise him with lute and harp!
> Praise him with timbrel and dance;
>   praise him with strings and pipe!
> Praise him with sounding cymbals;

> praise him with loud clashing cymbals!
> Let everything that breathes praise the Lord!
> Praise the Lord! (Ps. 150).

With all our being, with every breath, with the whole of creation, let us praise the Lord. He has not yet left us alone; he will not ever leave us alone.

5. Dealing with Our Frailty (vv. 13–18)

Like a father who knows that children are children and cannot be expected to be adults, God knows we are his children, not yet full grown. His pity is reserved for those who "fear him." "Fear" means to reverence him as God, to stand in awe of him as the Almighty. Leupold's translation, "has always pitied," [10] points to the Lord's long record of pardons freely bestowed.

He who made us knows us. "He" is emphatic. Word arrangement in the text requires a translation like this: "For he, even he, knows our frame." If anyone should understand the creature, it is the Creator. He remembers that we are "dust." We were fashioned of frail elements. Thus, we are frail. It is reassuring to know that our Maker knows that. We are perishable and temporal like the grass seared by the hot desert winds.

In contrast, the Lord's steadfast love is "from everlasting to everlasting." It stretches from eternity on one side to eternity on the other side with no gap in between. Man's life lasts but a little while. The Lord's love is forever. It is eternal for "those who fear him." His righteousness extends to "children's children." This means his gracious dealings project to the third generation, the grandchildren. Such love and righteousness at work in "those who fear" God will result in keeping his covenant and doing his commandments. Reverence results in obedience. God's abounding love stands out when compared with the frail, undeserving creature who receives it. The nation should bless God for national benefits.

Universal Praise, 103:19-22

1. Extensiveness of His Rule (v. 19)

In ever-growing concentric circles the call to praise God

has broadened. Before the summons was issued to all creation to join in the chorus of praise, the psalmist reminded us of the reach of the Lord's rule. God's realm is the totality of things, the entire universe. He rules over all.

He is not a narrow, national God, concerned only with Israel. His concern and lordship are as extensive as the universe. Sometimes we mistakenly assume that God is interested only in "spiritual" things or church things or big decisions. He is concerned with these. His sovereignty stretches over all such matters. Jesus is Lord of the church, but that doesn't exclude his lordship over the Christian beyond the life, programs, and activities of the church with which he is associated. For example, the Lord is interested in the tithe brought to the church; but he is equally Lord over the rest of the resources that are used for other personal and family things. He rules over all.

2. *Inclusiveness of the Call to Praise* (vv. 20–22)

"Angels" are ordered to praise God. They are accustomed to "do his word." The word translated "angels" is often rendered "messenger." Reference may be to heavenly messengers (angels, as we are accustomed to call them); or it may designate earthly messengers. The synonym for "angels" is "you mighty ones." The latter phrase translates a word which regularly refers to a man of war, a tough soldier. The word may point to a soldier in God's earthbound task force. Whoever these messengers were, they were responsive to the Lord's purposes. Notice what they did with his word. Emphasis is not on hearing it or on sharing it, but on doing it.

The "hosts" were encouraged to join in the chorus of blessing. "Hosts" may mean celestial bodies, like the earth, Mars, the sun, and the moon (Deut. 4:19). Or it may refer to the heavenly hosts, that army Elisha prayed that his servant might see (2 Kings 6:17). They are "servants" of God. They

Notes

INTRODUCTION

1. Kyle M. Yates, *Preaching from the Psalms* (Nashville: Broadman Press, 1948), pp. ix–x.
2. Leonard Griffith, *God in Man's Experience: the Activity of God in the Psalms* (Waco: Word Books, 1968), p. 13.
3. H. C. Leupold, *Exposition of the Psalms* (Grand Rapids: Baker Book House, 1975), p. 28.
4. Ralph Spaulding Cushman, "His Presence Came Like Sunrise," *The Best Loved Religious Poems,* comp. James Gilchrist Lawson (Old Tappan: Fleming H. Revell, 1933), pp. 147–148.

CHAPTER 1

1. J. B. Phillips, *Your God Is Too Small* (New York: The Macmillan Company, 1957), pp. 9–59.
2. Yates, p. 173.
3. Words by Horatius Bonar.
4. Griffith, p. 15.
5. Words by Horatius Bonar.

CHAPTER 2

1. Leupold, p. 399.
2. Ibid., pp. 404–405.

Chapter 3

1. Derek Kinder, "Psalms 73–150," *Tyndale Old Testament Commentaries* (London: InterVarsity Press, 1975), p. 260.
2. Rudolph Kittel, *Die Psalmen* (Leipzig: A. Deichertsche Veralgsbuchhandlung, 1922), p. 241.
3. W. O. E. Oesterley, *The Psalms* 2 (New York: The Macmillan Company, 1939), p. 344.

Chapter 4

1. Leupold, p. 363.
2. "He's Got the Whole World in His Hands," © 1952 Century Press.
3. Edwin McNeill Poteat, exposition, *The Interpreter's Bible* 4 (New York: Abingdon Press, 1955), p. 242.
4. William R. Taylor, exegesis, *The Interpreter's Bible* 4 (New York: Abingdon Press, 1955), p. 242.

Chapter 5

1. Taylor, p. 40.
2. Leupold, p. 84.
3. Ibid., p. 85.
4. Ibid., p. 86.

Chapter 6

1. Leupold, p. 237.
2. Ibid., p. 238.
3. John I. Durham, "Psalms," *The Broadman Bible Commentary* 4 (Nashville: Broadman Press, 1971), p. 226.
4. Taylor, p. 149.
5. Durham, p. 226.
6. Artur Weiser, "The Psalms," *The Old Testament Library* (Phila-

NOTES

delphia: The Westminster Press, 1962), pp. 253–254.
7. Durham, p. 226.

CHAPTER 7

1. Yates, p. 17.
2. Taylor, p. 170.
3. Leupold, p. 267.
4. Yates, p. 21.
5. Durham, p. 235.

CHAPTER 8

1. Leupold, p. 210.
2. Ibid., p. 211.
3. Author Unknown.
4. Author Unknown.
5. Leupold, p. 210.
6. "Fill My Cup, Lord," © 1959 Richard Blanchard; © 1964 Sacred Songs.

CHAPTER 9

1. Leupold, p. 715.
2. Taylor, p. 544.
3. Oesterley, p. 437.
4. Yates, p. 87.
5. Griffith, p. 99.
6. J. Wash Watts, *A Survey of Old Testament Teaching* 1 (Nashville: Broadman Press, 1947), p. 295.
7. Kinder, p. 365.
8. Ibid.
9. Yates, p. 90.
10. Leupold, p. 717.